A Treatise Upon Horsemanship, Tr. by W. Frazer

Fran##ois Robichon De La Gu##rini##re

A TREATISE

UPON

HORSEMANSHIP,

TRANSLATED FROM THE ORIGINAL FRENCH

OF

M. DE LA GUERINIERE,

Equerry to Louis the Fifteenth of France;

BY CAPTAIN WILLIAM FRAZER.

INCLUDING

BERENGER'S CHAPTERS ON BITTING, WITH THE EFFECT OF THE SNAF-
FLE AND RUNNING REINS, IN PLACING THE HEAD, AND PRESERVING
THE TEMPER OF YOUNG AND UNFORMED HORSES, AS PRACTISED BY
THE LATE

SIR SIDNEY MEADOWS.

TO WHICH ARE ADDED

Notes from the Earl of Pembroke's Military Equitation.

CALCUTTA:

PRINTED BY THOMAS HOLLINGBERY.

HIRCARRAH PRESS.

1801.

CONTENTS.

PREFACE.   PAGE.

CHAPTER I.
Of the Riding School,   -   -   -   I

CHAPTER II.
Of the various Tempers of Horses,   -   -   -   3

CHAPTER III.
Of the instruments used in dressing Horses, viz. the saddle, bridle, bridon, mar-tingale, cavefon, chambriere, switch, the spurs, the longe, and the pillars, - 6

CHAPTER IV.
Of the Terms of the Art,   -   -   -   39

CHAPTER V.
Of the different motions of the legs of a Horse in his several paces,   -   44

CHAPTER VI.
Of mounting and dismounting,   -   •   -   56

CHAPTER VII.
Of the Bridle-hand and its Effects,   -   -   66

CHAPTER VIII.
Of the Aids and Instruments necessary to dress Horses,   •   74

CHAPTER IX.
Of the necessity of the Trot to make a young Horse supple, and of the utility of the Walk,   .   -   :   80

CHAPTER X.
Of the stop, the half stop, and the reining back,   -   -   87

CONTENTS.

PAGE.

CHAPTER XI.

Of the Shoulder-in, - - - 94

CHAPTER XII.

Of the Croup to the Wall, - - 101

CHAPTER XIII.

Of the utility of the Pillars, - - - 108

CHAPTER XIV.

Of the Paſſage, - - - 113

CHAPTER XV.

The changes of hands and the manner of doubling, - 118

CHAPTER XVI.

Of the Gallop, - - - 121

CHAPTER XVII.

Of Volts, Demivolts, Paſſades, Pirouettes, and Terre a Terre, - 126

CHAPTER XVIII.

Of the High Airs, - - - 138

THE WAR HORSE, - - 153
THE HUNTER, - - - 157
OF CARRIAGE HORSES, - - 164

ERRATA.

Page 56, after line 12, inſert
CHAPTER VI.

PREFACE.

IT may be deemed proper to fay fomething on the publication of a Volume which has been fo long promifed to the public, and is now produced under the patronage of the MOST NOBLE THE GOVERNOR GENERAL, in the hope that it may prove acceptable to thofe who wifh to benefit by a fcientific theory of horfeman-fhip, and practice the rules, in fituations where they may not be able to procure the aid of a mafter.

Convinced of the great fuperiority of MONS. DE LA GUERI-NIERE's fyftem, and anxious to acquire knowledge upon every fubject that related to a favourite purfuit, I long ago tranflated his Treatife on the Stud; and had advanced a good way in that of his Riding School, when I underftood from CAPTAIN ISAAC HUM-PHRYS, that the late COLONEL THOMAS DEANE PEARSE, Commandant of the Bengal Artillery, had tranflated the fame Treatife, at the requeft of MR. HASTINGS.

The executors* of the eftate, with that degree of liberality which diftinguifhes men anxious to promote public purpofes, prefented me with the manufcript, which I prepared for the prefs, by col-lating it carefully with the original, and ftriking out thofe parts which appeared more calculated to encreafe the fize, than the utility, of the Volume. This, with the tranflation of his Treatife upon the Stud, I prefented to the HON. SIR JOHN SHORE, then Governor General, who propofed printing it at the public ex-

---

* Captains Ifaac Humphrys and Henry Grace.

pence, ordered the plates to be engraved, and four hundred copies to be ftruck off. By fome unaccountable means the manufcript was loft, and going over the work again, I perceived that BEREN-GER, in his tranflation of *Bourgelot* (a contemporary Parifian author) was, in feveral places, more full and fatisfactory than GUERI-NIERE; which induced me to propofe the prefent mode of arrangement.

This mode has happily met the approbation of the Moft Noble the MARQUIS WELLESLEY; and, as His Lordfhip has given the moft generous and flattering encouragement to my feeble endeavours, I have now only to hope, that thofe may prove as ufeful to the public, as I have found them inftructive to myfelf.

The Treatife being merely didactick, arranged in the fimpleft form, and expreffed in the plaineft language, little is required in the tranflation. Yet there are fome few words, the appropriate meaning of which, as applied to the Manege, I have not been able to find in any Dictionary; thefe however are unimportant, but the word *paffage* muft be particularly attended to; for, in the common Englifh acceptation, it means going to one fide; while the meaning, as applied by MONS. DE LA GUERINIERE, is the elevated, fhortened, cadenced walk, or trot, whether advancing, reining back, going to the right, or to the left; and upon one fpot it is termed piaffe.

A
TREATISE UPON
HORSEMANSHIP.

CHAPTER I.

OF THE

RIDING SCHOOL.

ALL the arts and fciences have rules and principles by means of which difcoveries are made that lead to perfection. Horfemanfhip feems to be the only one that requires nothing but practice, and this miftaken idea is the reafon why there are fo few well dreffed horfes, and why the greater part of thofe, who flatter themfelves they are horfemen, have fo little capacity.

The want of defined principles, puts it out of the fcholar's power to diftinguifh faults from perfections; he has no refource but imitation; and unfortunately it is more eafy to follow a bad example, than to acquire ufeful knowledge.

Meffieurs Du Pleffis, and de la Vallée, fo much efteemed in the happier days of horfemanfhip, have left us no rules to lead to that perfection which they acquired; deprived of thofe advantages, we can only feek for information, in the works of thofe, who have recorded the principles of their practice; and amongft an infinite number of more modern authors, there are only two, whofe works are held in general eftimation. Monfieur De La Broue, who lived in the Reign of Henry the fourth of France, compofed a work in folio, comprifing the principles and practice of his mafter John Baptifte Pignatelli, who taught in the academy of Naples, the beft fchool in the world, to which all the nobility of France and Germany, who wifhed to become perfect in the art of horfemanfhip, reforted, to benefit by the leffons of this illuftrious mafter.

The Duke of Newcaftle, an englifh nobleman, who was preceptor to Charles the fecond, paid the fcience of horfemanfhip the greateft of honours, by making it the ftudy of his whole life; and was allowed to be the moft fkilful horfeman of his age.

Amongft the other Italian, French, and German authors, who have written upon horfemanfhip; fome have been prolix and diffufe, others have been laconic and concife: both of thofe errors I fhall endeavour to avoid; and in the following fheets, deliver my ideas upon the fubject, fo as to be clearly underftood, with the affiftance of the plates, as a fubftitute for the fchool.

The opinions of thofe who attempt to ridicule the theory of the art, will not prevent me from maintaining it's utility. I agree however, that in an exercife where the body acts the principal part, practice is indifpenfably neceffary.

Theory teaches us to proceed upon juft principles, which inftead of oppofing, ferve to improve and embellifh nature.

Practice produces facility, in carrying into effect the fyftem, that theory inculcates; to acquire this facility, patience and affiduity, with decifion and vigour, but above all the love of horfes, is required; and thefe quali-ties conftitute a true horfeman. There are few men who do not love horfes; that fentiment feems to arife from gratitude for the fervice the animal renders man. Should any perfon think otherwife, the punifhment of his indifference will arife from the accidents he is expofed to, or from his being deprived of the fervice of that noble and valuable animal.

By vigour and decifion, I do not mean excefs of violence, or imprudent temerity, but that kind compulfive force, which keeps the horfe in awe of the aids and chaftifements; while his rider preferves that eafe, equilibre, and grace, infeparable from true horfemanfhip.—The difficulty of ac-quiring thefe qualities, and the length of time neceffary to become perfect in the art, has made many perfons (who affect to know a great deal) declare the manage ufelefs; thefe prejudices, which timid truth cannot al-ways oppofe with effect, prevent many from cultivating this noble and ufe-ful exercife, which tends to render a horfe fupple, mild, and obedient; without which, he muft be entirely unfit for war, the chafe, or the fchool.

————

CHAPTER II.

Of the various Tempers of Horfes.

This knowledge is the firft defideratum in the art, and every fcholar fhould make it his principal ftudy; but long experience is required, to en-able a horfeman to difcover the fources of good or bad difpofitions.

With a horfe of proper ftature and proportion of parts, inheriting ftrength, courage, and docility, the true principles of the fchool may rea-dily be put in practice; but when nature rebels, and the caufe of obftinacy is not perceptible, the means employed to fubdue, may create new oppofition, inftead of curing thofe vices fuppofed to be known.

Want of docility commonly proceeds from exterior or interior defects, weaknefs natural or accidental, in the reins, haunches, hoofs, fhoulders, legs, or the fight; want of courage, fluggifhnefs, impatience, paffion and malice, to which might be added bad habits.

Bad habits are occafioned by bad management, and when once rooted, they are more difficult to correct than a bad natural difpofition : Colts begin to contract them at a very early period, when at liberty in the ftud ; which makes it painful to them to fubmit to their firft leffons, and the dominion of mankind, who taking the advantage, which they pretend to affert nature has given them over horfes, too often carry their power beyond moderation ; and no animal has a ftronger fenfe, or more retentive memory of undeferved punifhment than a horfe.

Formerly there were people employed folely to train colts, when taken from the dam, denominated *Cavalcadours de Bardelle.* They were always chofen from amongft thofe diftinguifhed for patience, ingenuity, boldnefs, and diligence ; qualities not fo immediately neceffary amongft horfes that have been mounted ; their bufinefs was to handle and familiarize the colts, to take up their feet frequently, and beat the under part of the hoof gently in the manner of driving a nail ; to accuftom them to the bit, faddle, girths, and crupper, by which means they gained upon the colts, made them gentle and eafy to mount, never ufing force or coercion, until every other means failed. Thus they rendered every colt familiar and fond of man ; while his vigour, powers and courage were preferved. The adoption of fimilar practice in modern times would be found equally effectual.

Effential defects of dangerous confequence are fhynefs, vice, to be reftive, *ramingue* and *entier.*

Shyneſs proceeds from the fear of particular objects which they will not approach : this may ariſe from natural timidity, or a defect of viſion, which makes objects appear different from what they really are : this fault is encreaſed by beating. There are alſo ſome horſes, that after being long confined in the ſtable, will ſtart at every thing they ſee upon firſt coming out, but this is of very ſhort duration, if they are not beaten, and are with patience familiarized to ſtrange objects.

A vicious horſe is that which by ill uſage has become ſo perverſe, as to bite, kick, and hate his rider ; ignorant and ill-tempered horſemen, make their horſes vicious.

A reſtive horſe (ignorantly called a ruſty horſe) refuſesto go forward, ſtands ſtill in the ſame place, and reſiſts the efforts of his rider in different ways, the word is derived from the verb *reſter* to ſtop.

A *ramingue* horſe, in working doubts and heſitates to go forward, advances a little and then ſtops, and is as it were of two minds : the original word *ramingo* in Italian ſignifies a young bird or neſtling, which when full grown and fledged, refuſes to quit the neſt or bough, tho' urged and ſolicited by the parent birds to launch into the air and take its flight.

The *entier* horſe, refuſes to turn, and this proceeds from the awkward-neſs and ſtiffneſs of his body and limbs ; ſometimes however from vice and bad habits. The temper, or mind of the animal (if the expreſſion may be granted) muſt be ſoftened and ſoothed, or the pliancy of the limbs, will avail but little : they ſhould therefore act in concert, and as the one is able, the other ſhould be willing and ready. The term *entier* in its figurative ſenſe, in which it muſt be always underſtood in horſemanſhip, means a ſtiff-horſe, or one that is not ſuppled, and therefore refuſes to turn from the pain and difficulty which he finds in putting himſelf into a proper poſ-ture : in its original and literal ſignification, the word means whole, intire, unbroken, and is derived from the Italian word *intero* as that is from the Latin *integer* : the Italians therefore, who always fpeak in metaphor, and from whom the terms of horfemanfhip are adopted, or naturalized, by other nations, figuratively call a ftiff and undifciplined horfe an intire or unbroken horfe; which from the ftiffnefs and tightnefs of his joints and mufcles, is not able to bend himfelf, but in turning moves all of a piece, like a beam, or bar of iron; while the active and fuppled horfe, who can bend himfelf readily, and becomes part of the circle he defcribes in turning, may be faid to be like a chain, fo to loofen and fhift his limbs, as to break and divide himfelf as it were into parts: hence perhaps the term horfe breaker.

When thefe defects arife from want of courage, or from weaknefs, it will not be eafy to remove them by art. It is neceffary however to remark, that both the courage and powers of the animal may be deftroyed, by mounting, and dreffing, when too young. The proper age depends upon various circumftances of lineage, climate and individual qualities.

CHAPTER III.

Of the inftruments ufed in dreffing horfes, viz. the faddle, bridle, bridon, martingale, cavefon, chambriere, fwitch, the fpurs, the longe, and the pillars.

SECTION I.

The demipeak is perhaps the beft kind of faddle for young horfes and fcholars, but it fhould exactly fit the horfe, and be placed fo as neither to impede the motion of the fhoulders, nor throw the weight upon the loins; the pannel ſhould be equally ſtuffed, and may be advantageouſly lined with goat's ſkin, the hair outwards; if the horſe is well formed, neither crupper nor breaſt band will be required, though both are uſeful for troop horſes.

SECTION II.

THE BRIDLE.

1ſt. *The Mouth-piece.*

The *mouth-piece* in order to produce the wiſhed for effects, and operate juſtly and with certainty upon the mouth, ſo as to be able to raiſe, ſupport, unite or reſtrain the horſe, without violence or pain, ſhould be placed directly and evenly upon the *bars*, exactly between the teeth called the *grinders* and the *tuſhes*; and the chain called the *curb*, ſhould reſt equally and ſmoothly on that hollow under the chin, commonly called the beard. The *mouth-piece* by its *appuy*, or the force with which it preſſes the *bars*, is employed to retain the horſe in his pace, and to make him ſtop. The *branches* govern, direct, and unite him; and the *curb* is the cement and ſoul of both: for the *mouth piece* could have but little influence over the *bars* from above, nor the *branches* when pulled below, if the *curb* did not connect and animate both. This is the manner in which the bitt operates, by means of the parts which compoſe it, viz. the *mouth-piece, branches,* and *curb*, each of which has its diſtinct office, although all muſt concur and act in union, to produce the propoſed effect. We will explain how this end is to be attained, and, to be more exact, will ſpeak of each article ſeparately.

SECTION III.

The branches and curb, are formed in different fizes, in different fhapes and proportions, as the mouth which is to wear the bitt requires, and thefe different fhapes and proportions are what diftinguifh one bitt from another.

The *mouth-piece* is that part of the bitt which the horfe carries in his mouth: this is fometimes made of one intire piece of iron, *kneed* or bent in the middle, and fometimes quite ftrait. Some again have a joint in the middle, and other mouth-pieces have a hollow fpace in the middle, in which the tongue is lodged, which being not preffed fo much as when the mouth-piece is level, remains more free and undifturbed. This arched fpace is called the mounting, *liberty* or *upfet*; and from its fhape and fafhion, gives a particular denomination to the bitt, as a *pigeon* necked, a *duck* or *goofe* necked bitt; fo called, becaufe the two parts which compofe this neck are formed in refemblance of the necks of thefe birds. The *branches* are thofe parts of the bitt to which the *mouth-piece* is joined and inferted, and which reaches from the horfe's cheek to a certain length below his chin. They are fometimes bent and turned into different fhapes, and according to the proportion in which they are bent produce different effects upon the horfes mouth. When ftrait, the branches confift but of two parts; an *eye*, or hole at the top, to which the head-ftall is buckled; and an hole, or ring at the bottom, in which the reins are faftened; befides this, one or two fmall *chains*, and fometimes a flender bar of iron run acrofs near the bottom, to keep the *branches* firm and fteady.

Thofe *branches*, which are formed obliquely, are bent in different parts, and in different degrees at the upper end, near the mouth-piece. When they are bent fo as to make a projection near the *mouth-piece*, this projection is called the *elbow*, or *fhoulder*; and when it is towards the bottom, it is named the *knee* or *ham*. There is an imaginary line belonging to all bitts, called by horfemen and bitt-makers, the *line* of the *banquet,* or upper part of the branch above the mouth-piece, which beginning from the *eye* at the top of the branch, runs to the end. In this all the delicacy of the art confifts; for it is the rule and guide by which the bitt is to be adapted to the mouth, and by which the ftrength or weaknefs of the branches are to be known. To thefe we may add one part more, which is called the *arch of the banquet,* and is at the infertion of the *mouth-piece* into the branches. Under this, there is another called the *beard.*

The next and laft article belonging to the bitt, is the *chain,* or *curb,* which goes under the *chin.* The perfection of the bitt, and the certainty of its effects depend upon the union and correfpondence of the *curb* with the *branches.* To attain this purpofe, great exactnefs muft be obferved, as that it be of a juft and fuitable length with the *beard,* and that it remains flat and immoveable in its place, not galling, or pinching the part, but yet keeping it in due fubjection: for were it to be loofe, and fhift its place, it would render the branches entirely ufelefs. This *curb* is compofed of many links; the larger they are, the gentler and eafier they are, and when, from the ticklifhnefs and delicacy of fome horfes, they happen to be too ftrict, a piece of cloth or leather, put between them and the *beard,* will blunt their effect. The adjufting the *curb* properly, is a matter not only of the utmoft confequence to give the branches their due power, but is alfo of fo much exactnefs and nicety, that few of the bitt-makers themfelves are equal to the tafk, fo as to know the fhape and temper of each mouth, the dependence which all parts of the bitt have upon one another, of what length or fhape to form the *branches,* and to complete the machine with that truth and juftnefs, which the purpofe to which it is deftined moft abfolutely requires. The greateft difficulty is to fix the *curb*; and, although it calls for fo much care and knowledge, and almoft each horfe, from the fize or temper of his mouth, fhould wear his bitt *with*

C

a difference, yet they are generally kept *ready made*, and many people are content to buy them fo, and thruft them into their horfe's mouths, pleafed with the polifh, and mechanic neatnefs of the work, which in this nation is very beautiful; and judging this to be fufficient, concern themfelves no farther.

Of outward form elaborate, of inward lefs exact. MILTON.

When the *curb* (as already mentioned) is too loofe and long, it defeats the operation of the *branches*, and by giving too much room, allows them to go back, which pofture oftentimes galls and frets the horfe's lips, and frees him from fubjection to the hand.

When it is too fhort, it is always too fevere, and binds and gags the horfe, fo as to occafion great uneafinefs and difturbance, depriving the branches likewife, to a certain degree, of their juft effect. In order to hinder the *hook* to which the *curb* is hung, and which confines it in its place, from hurting the horfe either in his cheek or lip, great care fhould be taken to turn it fomewhat round and thick, and to proportion its length, fo that it may touch only the extremity of the lip, which is the place where it joins the laft link of the *curb*. The due length is generally fixed by the diftance from the *eye* of, the *branch*, to the *elbow*, or *fhoulder*; and in *ftrait* branches where there is none, to the *place* where the elbow *would* be, if there was one. If the *beard* is too tender and fenfible, it will be proper to make the *curb* of *one* piece of iron, remembering to have it round, fmooth, and well polifhed; taking care to make the curb reft in its place, and not to flip up above the *beard* upon the jawbone, as it happens to horfes which are fmall, narrow, and very quick of feeling in that part. To keep it fteady, therefore, the *hooks* muft be longer than they commonly are, hollow or arched, efpecially upwards, and the *curb* either round or flat, according as the *beard* requires, and *fhort*, to balance the extraordinary length of the *hooks*. To shield the *beard* likewise from the preffure of the *curb*, a bit of cloth, or leather, may be put between them ; and where the part is fo very ticklifh, as hardly to allow any thing to touch it, the *curb* may be made entirely of *leather.* There is likewife another method which may be practifed upon thefe occafions, either to work with the reins put under the *fhoulder* of the bitt, which leffens, to a great degree, the force of the *curb*, and is called working with falfe reins ; or elfe to lay the curb entirely afide. As thefe *curbs* are calculated for the eafe and relief of horfes whofe *beards* are too foft and yielding, there is a fort of *curbs* likewife which are deftined folely to horfes whofe *beards* are thick, flefhy, and fo dull and hard, as fcarcely to have any feeling, but lean upon the hand, *force*, or break from it, and commit many diforders, either from a bad temper, want of ftrength, of fupplenefs, and activity ; or, as it fometimes happens, of all together. The *curb* prefcribed for horfes of this character (having firft tried the fmooth *curb* of one piece) muft be hollow, indented, or armed with fmall teeth, and of one piece of iron.

This indeed has great power, and will perform all that can be executed by a bitt ; but it is too rude, and fo painful, as to be unbecoming in an horfeman to ufe. The more eligible part will therefore be, with horfes to which fuch feverity is requifite, either to reject them totally, or endeavour to form them by milder treatment, and with judgment and knowledge, rather than to expofe them, by the harfhnefs of this curb, to work difagreeably, or be indebted for their obedience to fo much rigour and cruelty. It was likewife cuftomary to fix above the *mouth-piece* a thin *chain*, or flender bar of iron, refembling a fmall *fnaffle*, but better known by the French term of *trenckefile.* This, at prefent, at leaft in this country, is laid afide ; it neverthelefs has its ufe, and may be employed with advantage to horfes which are apt to *drink* or *fwallow* their *bitt*, as the expreffion is, or bury it fo deep in their mouths, as to hinder it from having a due and juft effect. It ferves alfo, to a certain degree, as a *player*, to refrefh and enliven the mouth, fomewhat in the fame manner as the little chain fo called, which is hung in the middle of the *upfet*, and laying upon the tongue, keeps it in motion, and makes the mouth moift and pleafant.

Such, under various forms and combinations, are the component parts of the machines called *bitts*. The general rules which muft be obferved in adapting them to the mouth, the different forts at prefent in ufe, with their properties and effects, will now demand to be confidered; but as this cannot be done but relatively to the mouths to which they are to be applied, it will be indifpenfably neceffary, in this place, previoufly to fpeak of them, and of feveral particulars incident to them.

SECTION IV.

Of the Bars and Lips.

In order to be able to adjuft a bitt to the mouth of any horfe, the firft thing neceffary is to examine the qualities, and to confider and meafure the proportions, fo as to make it tally and anfwer to the temper and properties of each particular part. The method of doing this, is to be able to difcern the natural faults and imperfections, fo as to palliate and correct them by the ftructure of the bitt; for were the mouths of horfes good and perfect, there would be no trouble, and little need of fcience, to furnifh them with bitts.

The general defects are, that they are *too* narrow and fmall, or too large and wide; that they have the *tongue* too thick and broad; the channel, or place where it is lodged, too confined and ftraitened; the *bars* too dull and hard, or too delicate; the *lips* too flat and flefhy; the *palate*, or roof of the mouth, too nice and ticklifh, and too low, that is to fay too *flefhy*, or not fufficiently fo; and above all, the jaws too large, narrow, and confined. Nor does it fail fometimes to happen, in addition to the perplexity which each particular defect will occafion, that they all meet together in the fame horfe, and being oppofite and contrary to each other, will demand the utmoft fkill of the moft able horfeman to fteer between thefe difficulties, which this complication of diforders will throw in his way.

It is not, however, the thicknefs of the *lips*, the hardnefs of the *bars*, nor the bignefs of the *tongue*, which need occafion much trouble; for a palliative, if not a remedy, may certainly be found in allowing a large and open *liberty* to the bitt, fo as not to prefs or confine the tongue; and in having a firmer and fuller *appuy* upon the *bars*, but fo as not to fqueeze, or difturb the lips. But when the *mouth* is narrow, and the *bars* at the fame time tender, a more ferious diftrefs muft arife; for if the *mouth-piece* is fmall and thin, to fuit the fize of the mouth, it will offend and hurt the *bars*; and in this inftance, the *bitt*, inftead of fixing and affuring the horfe's head, will teaze and fret him fo as to make him tofs it about, and commit many diforders with it. When the *tongue* is grofs and clumfy, and the *channel* narrow, the *appuy*, or ftrefs of the *mouth-piece*, which ought to be upon the *bars*, will render the *liberty* fo comparatively fmall, that it will act rather upon the *tongue*; and, inftead of eafing and relieving, will confine and prefs upon it, fo as to occafion uneafy fenfations. Again, when the *tongue* is unreafonably large, and the *palate* very low, and quick of feeling, the *liberty*, being required to be very high, will rub and fret the *palate* with its top, fo as to make the horfe open his mouth in a difagreeable manner, *beat* upon the hand, and behave very irregularly. Thefe difficulties every horfeman muft expect to encounter; and they are fo combined and united, as to require the utmoft fkill and difcernment to reconcile them together; nor will the beft efforts, and niceft refinements of the arts fucceed, without much patience, continu-

D

ed exercife, and the difcreteft conduct. It has been already mentioned, that the fenfibility, or dulnefs of the *bars*, proceed from the greater or lefs quantity of flefh with which they are covered; as well as from their *form*, and their being more or lefs round, or *fharp* and *ridgy*, and fituated *high* or *low*. In proportion, therefore, to thefe qualities, it will follow, that the influence of the bitt, or *appuy*, muft be ftronger, or more gentle and moderate. Mere common fenfe inftructs us fo far; but we fhall be ftill more fully convinced by the horfe; for he muft neceffarily be guilty of many follies and extravagancies, when the bitt is either fo rude as to give him pain, or fo eafy and weak as to be ineffectual.

Thofe, horfes whofe mouths are good in all their qualities, and juft in all their parts; that is, whofe *mouths* are reafonably wide, whofe *tongue* lays eafily and properly in its channel, whofe *lips* are not thick, nor flefhy, whofe *bars* are endued with a certain degree of feeling, without being too tender, fuch horfes will require but little trouble, and the fimpleft and plaineft bitt will fuffice, efpecially if to thefe advantages, a fine and long *foreband*, a fmall and well-turned *head* be added, and they are active, ftrong, and gentle, with fpirit and courage; horfes of this ftamp will prevent the labours of art, for nature may almoft be faid to have *bitted* them herfelf, when fhe furnifhed them with thefe happy and fuperior qualities. The only difficulty is to find them.

When an horfe poffeffes all the qualities which conftitute a fine mouth, and, at the fame time, is weak in his fore parts, it is certain that he will, and muft lean more upon the hand than he ought, and will, upon this account, require a ruder and more powerful bitt; and although no bitt fhould be fo harfh as to caufe pain, yet, in this inftance, it is evident, that one ought to be ufed which is ftricter, and more compulfive, than in other circumftances would be neceffary.

When the *bars* are round and callous, and the lips are flefhy and big, the bitt fhould be fo conftructed, as to keep clear of the *lips*, and prefs only upon the *bars*. If, on the contrary, the *bars* are good, and the *lips* in fault, the intention of the bitt fhould be to eafe the *bars*, and attack the *lips* more forcibly. Both thefe are effected, by making the mouth-piece thicker or thinner, where it is to eafe, or prefs upon thefe parts. If the *bars* are hard and callous, and the lips fmall and thin; a *mouth-piece* fomewhat fharp and edged will be more effectual than one that is round. When the *bars* are hard, the *lips* large, or the mouth narrow, the *mouth-piece* fhould be formed fo as to affect the *bars*, and leave the *lips* at liberty; that is to fay, it fhould be thick and round at the middle, and fmaller and fharper at the end. When the mouth is dry and dull, a *player*, or fome rings hung upon the *mouth-piece*, by their turning and motion, will awaken the feelings, and make the mouth frefh and pleafant; and when the *bars* are fomewhat life-lefs, and the mouth narrow, fo as not to fuffer much iron to be put into it, a large *liberty*, with the *mouth-piece* narrowed, and fharpened off towards the ends, will take up lefs room, and from its fharpnefs be more felt by the *bars*. It muft be remembered, that each of thefe bitts muft have the liberty in proportion to the fize and action of the *tongue*, and the properties of the *palate*.

But when, to thefe imperfections, heat and fretfulnefs of temper are added; if the bitt, which was calculated to remedy the vices of the mouth only, fhould fail of the expected effect, inftead of augmenting its rigour, you fhould make it more eafy and gentle, by compofing the *mouth-piece* of one entire piece, without a *liberty*, if the *tongue* will permit; and if not, one fhould be made, ftill keeping the *mouth-piece entire*, that is to fay, not broken or disjointed, and the two parts faftened by a *link* in the middle; but the *liberty* hollowed out of a folid piece, which will have this advantage, that being folid, it will not bend, and will keep the mouth in a firm and juft *appuy*, fixing the *head*, and maintaining a conftant and equal degree of subjection in such horses as are apt to have their heads fickle and uncertain; and reconciling them to the constraint better than a *jointed liberty* could effect; teaching them, at the same time, by the uniformity of repeated lessons, that all their efforts of resistance are in vain, and that no irregular motions of the head, no grimaces, or distortions can avail, to change or remove what is fixed and stable; and to which habit and patience will, soon or late, dispose them to submit.

With respect to horses whose *bars* are high, sharp, and endowed with such sensibility, as scarcely to suffer any thing to touch them, a plain and simple mouth-piece, or *cannon* will be most suitable; it should be moulded likewise with the ends *thick* and *full*, and with a *liberty* for the tongue, which, by being bent, will work more upon the *lips*, and consequently spare the *bars*; while time and perseverance, which conquer most difficulties, will lend their assistance, and reconcile all. To proceed; it is not only necessary that the *branches* should have their peculiar and distinct effect, and that the *mouth-piece* should correspond with the structure and temper of the mouth; but it is indispensibly necessary, that both these parts should act together, and assist each other, and that with the utmost truth and exactness, otherwise many disorders would arise; for how nicely soever the *mouth-piece* may be adapted to the mouth, it will avail but little if the *branches* do not correspond; for if they are too rude and harsh, the horse will be afraid of the *mouth-piece*, gentle as it may be, as much as if it was really severe; and if, on the other side, the *branch* should be strait to a certain degree, and the *mouth-piece* too weak and easy, it would not have its due effect, to raise, confine, or support the horse; but he would lean upon the hand, and grow so heavy and dead, as to be very aukward and unpleasing. In these delicate circumstances the horseman must trust to his experience, and employ his judgment; nor is it a small share of either that will be sufficient to direct his conduct: above all, he should be well and intimately acquainted with the faults and defects of the horfe, and able to difcern when they will admit of a remedy, and when they are incurable; fhould know the temper, and fee what qualities nature has given, and what fhe withholds, fo that he may decide how far to interfere, and to what degree of juftnefs and grace he may hope to bring the animal, fo as to make it anfwer the end he wifhes to attain.

SECTION V.

Of the Tongue and Palate.

When the *tongue* is fo thick that it cannot be contained in the *channel,* or is too broad and big, it will prevent the *mouth-piece* from refting upon the *bars,* will make the *appuy* hard and dead, deprive the bitt of its due effect, and frequently be bruifed, fretted, and injured by it. The true and only remedy for thefe evils, is to allow a proper place for the tongue, by making a juft and convenient *liberty.* The fantaftical and ftrange *liberties* or *upfets* of bitts ; which are fo frequent in books, as well as the pre-pofterous bitts which are to be found in them, are entitled to no notice upon this occafion, inafmuch that they appear to have been formed rather to exercife the fancy and invention of the bitt-makers, than to anfwer the wants of the able and judicious horfeman.

In what cafes this *liberty* fhould be formed, either *whole,* or compofed of *two parts,* we have fet forth in the preceding chapter; it will be fufficient then barely to repeat in this, that when the *tongue* is well-formed, and of a reafonable fize, it fhould be fmall and moderate; and when the tongue is grofs and big, it fhould be large and fpacious; or, in other words, it fhould be adapted to the tongue, and made in meafure and proportion to it, care

E

being taken at the fame time, that it be not fo wide, as to affect the *bars*, for upon them the whole virtue of the bitt depends.

When the mouth is *fmall* and *narrow*, the *mouth-piece* muft be in proportion, remembering, at the fame time, that it fhould not be fo little and thin, as by its fharpnefs to alarm the *bars*; for it will be better to fuffer fome light temporary inconveniencies, fuch as to let it wrinkle the *lips*, or prefs upon the tufhes a little in the beginning, than to make the horfe defperate, by hurting the fenfibility of his bars; or, to avoid that fault, by putting more iron in his mouth than nature allows it to contain. With thefe difficulties the horfeman muft contend awhile; which, if attacked with prudence and moderation, will by degrees grow lefs and lefs, till they totally vanifh. Time, and a judicious treatment, will bring the bars to a proper tone and feeling, and the mouth will become at laft fo feafoned, as to be patient of the bitt, and obey its impreffions at the will of the hand which directs it.

To thefe likewife many faults and irregularities in the horfe may be added; as *gaping*, or opening the mouth beyond meafure, than which nothing is more difpleafing to the eye, *putting* out the *tongue*, or letting it hang out on *one fide*; *drawing* it up above the *mouth-piece*, *wreathing* and *moving his jaw*, *arming* himfelf, or refting the branches of the bitt, or his chin, upon his breaft, and carrying his head entirely on one fide; to thefe bad habits and tricks, it is not in the power of a bitt to furnifh a remedy. Long and patient exercife, difcretion, and a correct and judicious hand, are the only means which can be employed to redrefs thefe capricious poftures of the *head*; and for the opening of the mouth, the beft correction is to place the *nofe-band* low, and draw it very clofe and tight, unlefs the vice proceeds from the *bitt*, by being too big for the mouth, or caufing any pain or uneafinefs; in which cafe, the bitt muft be altered, and the caufe being removed, the effect will ceafe.

When the horfe *lolls out* his tongue, it proceeds either from a bad habit, or becaufe it is too *long*. When the latter is the cafe, it may be cut fhorter, and the remedy is certain, but too cruel to be offered, although conftantly prefcribed by ancient writers : when it is owing to mere whim and inclination, and the bitt fits fo juftly and equally in his mouth, that nothing can be found amifs, the fault muft either be permitted, or the offending part be made *fhorter* by *amputation*, as in the inftance of its being too long. When the horfe lolls it out on one fide, he thereby fruftrates, in part, the effect of the bitt, and renders the *appuy* uncertain. Frequent and gentle ftrokes of the fwitch or whip, to alarm and furprize him, are the beft corrections that can be ufed; though fome prefcribe a fort of *muzzle*, with fmall, and fharp points of iron, to prevent or punifh the fault. The horfes which draw up their tongues, and bring it over the *mouth-piece*, are generally guilty of this trick from heat, fretfulnefs, and too much fenfibility. To cure this evil, care fhould be taken that the bridle does not moleft or incommode the mouth; and that the *liberty* be fo eafy and large, as in no degree to prefs or difturb the tongue; and in order to pacify and moderate a temper too quick and impetuous, the lenities of patience and gentlenefs, of a light and fteady hand, and of a foft and eafy bitt, will prove the moft effectual medicines which can be adminiftered.

When an horfe turns and twifts his under jaw, being guilty of (as already faid) what the French horfemen term, *faire les forces*, or imitating the action of a pair of *fheers* when they cut any thing; the beft remedy is to ufe a bitt formed of *one* piece, and now and then to ftrike the part lightly with the whip, and keep a conftant hand. The horfe which is apt to *carry low*, or *arm himfelf*, which is effected by the horfe's curling his neck, fo as to touch the upper part of his throat with the branches of the bitt, commits a fault which is beyond the power of the bitt to prevent or cure. To hinder the habit of *arming*, a round bit of wood has been recommended by ancient writers, to be placed in the hollow part of the jaws, which, in some degree may stop his chin from turning downwards, so as to touch his throat, and prove more effectual than any affistance that can be gained from the bitt; which is a machine whose sole intention and sole powers are directed to pull the head *downwards*, and consequently cannot *raise* and *support*, and *pull it down*, at the same time. The usual method of attempting to raise the head, is to employ a bitt with branches that are easy and soft in their operation; or to make use of a bridoon to hold the hand high; but all these endeavours go but a little way, and are so very unequal to the task required, that those horsemen who undertake to raise an horse by the agency of the *bitt*, defeat their wishes by the very means they use to make them successful.

Having thus discoursed of *bitts* in a summary and general manner, it will, perhaps, be requisite, before we dismiss the subject, to recapitulate the foregoing particulars, and lay down the plainest and most certain rules for the information of those persons, who may wish to be acquainted with the properties of different bitts, and to know how to adapt them so as best to answer the horseman's views and intentions.

The easier, simpler, and lighter a bitt is in all its parts, provided it produces the desired effect, the better, and more agreeable it will be.

The neater and smaller the mouth-piece is, in proportion to the size and qualities of the mouth, the more pleasing it will be to the horse.

The mouth-piece that is made of two parts, and joined in the middle, is more easy than that which is whole and entire.

The rounder and fuller it is towards the *ends*, the softer and gentler it will be to the mouth.

The *liberty* or *upfet* fhould be formed in *proportion* to the mouth, efpe-cially to the *tongue*, for the eafe and accommodation of which it is prin-cipally calculated.

The *mouth-pieces*, called *pigeon-necks, goofe-necks, cats-feet, pas d' ane, canon a trompe*, or a *canne*, both which are entire, and *arched* in the middle, (and for which there is no Englifh term) with many others, are diftinguifh-ed from one another, only by being whole, or elfe of two parts jointed in the middle, being fuller and fmaller in the mouth, and by having the *upfet*, or *liberty*, larger or more confined.

In this particular, and in this only, the real and effential difference con-fifts, and not in the fantaftical figures and fhapes into which they are wrought, nor by the addition of *melons, bells, pears, balls, olives, pater-nofters*, or beads, *fcatch mouths*, and *cats-feet*, &c. with which, till of late years, it was ufual to cover and load the bitts; and which are now de-fervedly rejected, as cumberfome, abfurd, and ridiculous.

SECTION VI.

Of the effect of the Bridle.

It is from the *branches*, in alliance with the *curb*, that the *mouth-piece* receives all its life and power. Thefe branches act with greater, or lefs force, in proportion as they are nearer, or farther removed from that part of the *mouth-piece* which preffes upon the *bars*, and is the effence of the whole. With refpect to the line of the *banquet*, or upper end of the branch, and the *eye*, it muft be remembered, that the lower parts of the branch are influenced folely by the different proportions and different fituations of the upper part called the *eye*. If this is placed *high*, it re--

F

fifts the power of the branches, and keeps them ftrait and firm; fo that when they are pulled, the *mouth-piece*, which is between it and them, preffes more ftrongly upon the *bars*, than it would do, if either of thefe parts were to yield and give way to the other. On the contrary, if the *banquet* and *eye* were placed *low*, they would be too weak to refift the force of the *branches*, and the *mouth-piece* could have no effect. This is fo infallibly certain, that the fituation alone of the *eye* will make *branches* of different conftructions, operate in the fame manner, and produce the fame effect; fo that a ftrait *branch* will be as powerful, as one which is *bent* and turned, provided the *eye* be placed equal high in both: and the line in which the reins act, that is from the *ring* of the branch to which they are faftened, be equally diftant from the point of *appuy*, or that part of the *mouth-piece* before defcribed, which the branches immediately attack: the variety, therefore, of *turned* branches, which abounded formerly, and of which fome are ftill in ufe, are, perhaps, more to be commended for their graceful appearance, than for poffeffing any qualities fuperior to thofe inherent in the *ftrait*; for the powers of both depend upon the *eye*, which fits as fovereign, and commands the whole bitt. When the *eye* is fixed to a certain degree of *height*, and the branches are *fhort*, the bitt becomes powerful and fevere. The fituation being changed, and the *eye* lower, accompanied with a *long branch*, will make the bitt fofter, and more indulgent.

Long branches, by being at a diftance from the hand, confine and bring down the horfe's head; *fhort* branches, therefore, being nearer to the hand, muft contribute to raife it.

A branch, of whatever fhape it may be, becomes ftrong and rigorous, when the lower ends advance upon the *outfide* of the *line* of the *banquet*.

The contrary effect is obtained, by making the lower ends turn *inward*, or, in other words, *towards* the neck of the horse, as the term *outward* signifies *from* it.

Short branches are more forcible, and rougher than *long*, as their power is more instantly felt, than if it came from a distance, and awe and constrain the mouth very strictly.

Having thus *dissected* the bitt, and shewn the distinct and separate office of each part, we will now beg leave to gather up the scattered limbs, put them together, and place the entire machine in the horse's mouth.

SECTION VII.

Of the Bitt which should be given to a young horse.

In the beginning of an undertaking, whose aim is to subdue and reclaim nature, and that at a time when she is wild, ignorant, and even astonished at the attempts which are made upon her, it is evident that she must not be treated but with lenity, instructed with patience, and by small degrees, and that nothing should be offered that may hurt, surprize, or occasion any disgust. The horseman, therefore, should not act the part of a *tyrant*, but the part of a *lover*; not endeavour to *force* her submission, but strive to gain her *consent* and good will, by assiduity, perseverance, and the gentlest attentions; for what prospect of success would rougher manners afford? To what purpose would it be to compel a colt to go forward, or turn from fear of the whip or spur, and to trot and gallop so freely, as to supple his limbs, and form his paces, if the novelty of the bitt, and the unaccustomed restraint to which it subjects him, should vex and confound him, so as to make him not know what to do, nor how to behave in these extremes. It cannot be expected that he will be guided, and go with eafe to himfelf or pleafure to the rider, if the inftrument by which he is to be conducted offends, or gives him pain: all habits and acquirements fhould be attained gradually, and almoft imperceptibly; rigour and precipitation would ruin all, and inftead of forming the horfe to the execution of what is required, may plunge him into vice and rebellion, fo as to occafion much trouble and lofs of time before he can be reduced.

He fhould not, therefore, at firft be confidered as if he was defigned to be formed to all the exactnefs and delicacy of the bitt; and the horfeman fhould be content if he will endure it in his mouth, fo as to grow by little and little accuftomed to it, till the reftraint becomes by habit fo familiar and eafy, that he not only is not offended, but begins even to delight in it. For this purpofe great care fhould be taken, that the bitt be eafy and gentle in all its parts; that the *mouth-piece* be larger than it need be for an horfe already *bitted*; that it in no wife incommodes the *bars,* fqueezes the *lips,* or galls the *tongue.*

The mouth-piece called a *canon,* with a *joint* in the middle, will be the moft fuitable; the *ends* of it fhould be as large and full as the fize of the *mouth* will permit, for the thicker and more blunted they are, the eafier they will be to the horfe, and the *appuy* lefs ftrict and fevere. The links of the *curb* fhould be big, fmooth, and well polifhed; the *curb* fomewhat long; the *branches* fhould be exactly even with the *line of the banquet,* to make the *appuy* moderate and equal. They fhould likewife be *long*; nor does it fignify of what fhape they are, for with moft horfes, they ought to be fo weak, as fcarcely to have any effect; fo requifite it is to guard againft every thing that may annoy, or difturb the horfe in thefe firft trials. In order to reconcile him to this new conftraint, the reins fhould be held in both hands, and the horfe, for fome time, fhould only walk under the rider. Above all, upon this and all other occafions, a firm, a light, and diligent hand is neceffary; for although the bitt is as the *rudder*, by which the horfe is to be fteered, yet it is the *hand* which muft hold and direct the *rudder*; and fo fuperior is its power, that at all times it can make a gentle bitt *fevere*, and convert rigour to *eafe* and *foftnefs*.

Such are the *outlines*, and general principles upon which the art of bitting horfes is eftablifhed, and by which it muft exift. Under thefe heads, however, many diftinctions muft be made, and many variations permitted, which, however minute and nice, are yet fo effentially neceffary, that without attending to them upon proper occafions, the wifhes of the horfeman could never be accomplifhed.

It is not eafy, however, to defcribe and explain the *exceptions* to thefe general rules, becaufe they cannot always be forefeen, nor is it certain that they may happen; whenever, therefore, a cafe occurs in which a departure from thefe principles becomes neceffary, it muft be left to the judgment of the horfeman to act as the occafion requires; for no general and pofitive directions can be given in many unexpected difficulties which may arife, and which, therefore, the horfeman himfelf muft redrefs upon the fpot.

To attempt to point out the means of doing this in a book, would be acting like a phyfician, who prefcribes without feeing the patient; a bare reprefentation of the difeafe may indeed be made, but there may be many circumftances and particularities in the conftitution, which ought to be confidered, but which cannot be known till the parties are together. In our inftance, therefore, the patient *muft minifter to himfelf*, and act from his own knowledge and difcernment. The leading and general rules may be gathered from books, but the deviations from them to certain degrees, and the *refinement* of the art can be known and learnt only *among horfes*, and in the *manege*. I have, therefore, judged it to be the better part, to lay before the reader only

G.

a general view, without going into too minute a detail, which would probably avail only to puzzle and miſlead. For this reaſon I have likewiſe forborne to ſpeak of the bitts at preſent moſt in uſe; ſuch as the *conſtable* bitt, ſo called from the famous *Montmorency*, Conſtable of *France*, who was the inventor of it. The *French* bitt, the *Pignatelli* bitt, which bears the name of the renowned horſeman who firſt deſigned it. The *piſtol* bitt, or *buade*, owing its firſt name to its reſemblance of a piſtol in its *branches*, and the ſecond to its au_thor. Theſe, and a few others now in uſe, are to be ſeen in the ſhop of every bitt-maker, and their properties are explained in almoſt every treatiſe of mo_dern horſemanſhip.* Suffice it to repeat, that however they may vary in the ſhapes and figures of their *branches*, yet the eſſential difference conſiſts merely in their *length* or *ſhortneſs*, and in their being more or leſs *before* or *behind* the banquet, or in an *even* line with it.

Upon theſe foundations is erected the art of bitting horſes, which art, as far as it reaches, is ſure and conſtant; but which, in ſpite of all the merit and praiſe of which it has ſo long been in poſſeſſion, will, upon a ſerious and ſtrict trial, never, I doubt, be found adequate to the views of a ſound and intelligent horſeman, nor capable of bringing an horſe to that degree of ſup_pleneſs, and exactneſs of carriage, which the truth and perfection of the art require. Theſe attainments ſeeming to have been reſerved for a more ſimple, but powerful machine, called the *ſnaffle*.

---

* It is not for the ſame reaſon that the bitts uſed and valued in this nation, and diſtinguiſhed by the names of *Weymouth* bitts, *Pelham* bitts, *hard* and *ſharps*, &c. are not mentioned here. They are neither *bitts* nor *ſnaffles*, but *infra claſſem*, and of no account. Nor can what is called the Turkiſh bitt be valued, till ſeverity and brutal violence ſhall be deemed virtues in riding.

SECTION VIII.

Of the Snaffle.

From what has been said in the foregoing chapter, the reader muft be fenfible of the many difficulties which, from the difference of conformation in the *bodies* and *limbs* of horfes, the qualities of their *mouths*, their tempers, the fetting on of the *head*, and other particulars, that perfon has to encounter who undertakes to *bitt* an horfe. The almoft infinite *number* of bitts, which formerly were in ufe (but now judicioufly reduced to a very few), their variety of fhapes and figures, the ufe of *cavefons*, of *bridons* and *martingales*, which acted with them as auxiliaries, and the number of general rules and directions fummed up in the former chapters, all feem to proclaim the art of bitting an horfe to be one conftant ftruggle between nature and art; in which the former, though harraffed and reftrained, has feldom, I fear, been totally fubdued, and that from the infufficiency of the arms which have been employed againft her. The bridle, in its collective fenfe, is that inftrument, which principally enables the horfeman to govern and guide the horfe, fo as to make him execute what he requires of him. To perform his bufinefs juftly and gracefully, the animal muft firft be made very fupple in his fore parts; and his *head* and *neck* fo managed, that one may be *raifed*, and the other arched or *bent*, more or lefs, to the hand to which he is to turn. The bridle called the *bitt* is fo impotent in its endeavours to *raife* the head, that it even produces the oppofite effect; nor, from the confinement in which it keeps the horfe, and the fmall compafs it affords for the action of the rein, does it allow the rider fufficient room to bend him, without *pulling down* his head, and putting him upon his *fhoulders*, both of which are incompatible with the true and found principles of the art. The frequent ufe of *cavefons* and *bridons* fully evinces the want of power in the bitt to fupple the horfe, or raife the fore part.

The figures and reprefentations of horfes working upon different leffons may be appealed to, for the confirmation of this affertion; the books of paft times abound with them, efpecially the boafted work of that king of horfemen, the duke of Newcaftle; whofe horfes are all drawn with their heads between their knees, and yet are exhibited to the equeftrian world, as ftandards of truth, and models of perfection. The fucceffors of this duke, and of other great mafters, as imitators are generally a blind and fervile herd, ran head-long into the errors, adopted the faults of their predeceffors, and always made ufe of bitts, without reflecting upon their effects, or perceiving that they could operate but to make the horfe *carry low*, and to put him upon his *fhoulders*, while they thought he was all the time upon his *haunches*. And it is plain from the conftant ufe of bitts, and of *cavefons* in conjunction with them, that the ancient horfemen underftood but very imperfectly the pofture in which the horfe's head fhould be placed, fo as to influence and direct his motions according to the formation of his body and limbs; for there is fuch an immediate and ftrict connection and dependency between the parts, that the change of pofture in any fingle one, will more or lefs, affect the whole. To illuftrate this, let the horfe be confidered as a *lever*, or poll, when one end is *downward*, or towards the ground, it is certain that the other muft be *raifed* and turned upward. If the head of the horfe, therefore, is brought *down* towards his knees, it will follow that his *croupe* muft be *raifed*, and that it is then impoffible for him to be balanced upon his haunches, or to be well in *hand*; for the hand can have but little power over the horfe, while the head is *down*; nor has the horfe, when in this attitude, a poffibility of *uniting*, or *putting him-felf together*; for this can only be done, by bringing his *haunches* under him, and making them fupport the fore parts: a *bitt*, therefore, operating chiefly to bring *down* the head, cannot but, more or lefs, be the fource of thefe errors and contradictions. The ufe of the *bridon* joined with the *bitt* (unlefs confidered as a bridle *in referve*, in cafe the bitt fhould break, or otherwife fail), proves the infufficiency of the bitt to raife and fupport the fore parts. This little inftrument ferving only to awaken and animate the mouth, and raife the head when the horfe becomes heavy in the hand, or *carries low.*

The prodigious variety of *bitts* which were ufed in former times, loudly proclaim the difficulty of adapting thefe machines to the mouths of horfes, fo as to anfwer the wifhes of the rider; for although much wantonnefs was indulged in the invention of *fo many,* and of fuch ftrange forms; the greater part of them muft neverthelefs be confidered as purely calculated for the fervice of the horfeman; while the prodigious number of them, and the difference of their figures and dimenfions, prove the uncertainty of the means employed.

To form a conjecture of the intentions of the ancient horfemen from the bitts they ufed, they feem to have had little more in view than to awe and command the horfes by force and violence, fo as to be mafters of them at all events; and the bitts which they put into their mouths, and the *cavefons* over the nofe, plainly confefs that they placed all their hopes in the feverity of their tools, and the ftrength of the hand which held them; while all fenfibility in the horfe, and exactnefs and delicacy in the man, were either difregarded, or unknown. Thefe reproaches, however, are now no more, and the prefent times are fo enlightened, as to poffefs the art of bitting horfes in its fulleft extent, and to be able to difplay it in its utmoft force, purity, and elegance: unfortunate and miftaken at the fame time! For the *bitt,* with all its improvements and boafted virtues, can never operate fo as to reconcile *reftraint* with *liberty, raife* and *bend* at the fame time, fo as to draw up, and place the horfe's head and neck in a pofture which muft oblige him to be upon his haunches, without *boring* however, or turning his *nofe* upward, but in proportion to his ftructure and mould, keeping the mouth cool and frefh, and enabling the horfe to perform his bufinefs, be it what it will, with that

H

freedom, brilliancy, and juſtice, which conſtitute the perfection of horſemanſhip; unleſs, perhaps, in the inſtances of a few horſes, which may be ſo perfect in mind and body, as to be properly called the Phœnixes of their kind.

An humbler, plain, and hitherto deſpiſed inſtrument, can nevertheleſs do
the feat; and that with ſuch certainty, readineſs, and eaſe, that to prefer a *bitt*
to it, ſeems to be as ſtrange, as to make uſe of the huge, complex, and intricate
machine, called by the ingenious *Hogarth* *, a *new invention* to draw a cork out
of a bottle, inſtead of a common *ſcrew*; than which, in a good hand, nothing
can be more effectual.

This inſtrument is called the *ſnaffle*; and if ever there was a *panacea*, or
univerſal medicine, the *ſnaffle* is one for the mouths of horſes; it ſuits all, it
accommodates itſelf to all, and either finds them good, or very ſpeedily makes
them ſo; and the mouth once *made*, will always be faithful to the hand, let
it act with what agent it will. This bridle can at once ſubject the horſe to
great reſtraint, or indulge it in eaſe and freedom; it can place the head exactly
as the horſeman likes to have it, and work and bend the neck and ſhoulders to
what degree he pleaſes. He can raiſe the head, by holding up his hand; by
lowering it, it will be brought down; and if he chuſes to fix and confine it
to a certain degree, he muſt uſe for this, as well as for the purpoſe of *bending*,
double reins, that is, two on each ſide; the ends of which muſt be faſtened in
a ſtaple near the pommel of the ſaddle, or to the *girtbs*, higher or lower, as
the mouth, proportions of the horſe, and his manner of going require; and
if properly meaſured and adjuſted, they will form and command the horſe ſo
effectually, as in a great degree to palliate many imperfections of the mouth,
and many faults in the mould and figure.

The reins thus faſtened, or even *one* only, for the ſake of working one jaw
and ſide, will operate, more or leſs, as the *branches* do to a bitt, and the

---

* Vide his prints of the Rake's Progreſs.

snaffle will almost be a *bitt*, a *bridon*, a cavefon, and martingale in one. When the horseman would bend his horse, he must pull the rein of that side to which he is going, and lengthen that of the opposite, that they may not counteract each other. Nothing will awaken a dull mouth, and bring it to life and feeling, so soon as this bridle. If the mouth is hard and callous, the iron should be twisted so as to have a sort of edge, which will search the lips, and when they will permit, the *bars*; and if gently moved, or drawn from side to side, keep the mouth fresh and cool. If the *twisted*, or rough snaffle, is thought too harsh, and the hand not skilful enough to moderate its effects, a smooth snaffle may be used; or if a bit of linen be wrapped round the twisted snaffle, it will make it easy and smooth, and the mouth once made fine and delicate, will be true to its feelings, will obey the *snaffle*, and follow the hand with as much exactness and precision as the *bitt* knows to demand, but with more freedom and boldness than it ever can allow. Nor need the *aids* of the horseman be ruder, or more apparent, than when using a bitt; for if the horse be quick in his feeling, has a mouth well-worked and seasoned, and is active, supple, and willing, that is to say, be *completely dressed*, the rider may turn and wind him at pleasure, with as much grace, ease, and secrecy, as the bitt can boast. To conclude, the *bitt* is certainly more graceful, and the horse appears, when furnished with it, to more advantage; it likewise is more strong and coercive than the *snaffle*; but its power can be wanted only in the circumstances of hard mouths, and rude hands, where mere violence is preferred to gentleness and art; as in the instance of coach-horses, and many others, under the management of common grooms, and other ignorant people.*

---

* To the late Major General John St. Leger I am indebted for the following concise and valuable observations upon Sir Sidney Meadows's practice in dressing horses.

Begin by endeavouring to gain the confidence of your horse, in the stable, in the school, and in the field, which is easily done with a colt, or a horse that has not been ill treated, and may be effected in almost every case, by a man who possesses sagacity, patience, and courage, to discern his disposition, indulge his propensity, and command his obedience.

Although the running rein judiciously applied, will be found adequate to every case that can occur, in forming the mouth, and placing the head; it should be a general rule in training colts, to keep the head high: the vertebræ of a horse have been compared to

To such persons I do not address this discourse; yet I could tell them, if they wish to know, that it is the mouth alone in which they should put their trust, and not in the strength of their arms, nor in the rigour of the bitt; and when this is formed, and reduced to a just temper, and the hand knows how to *play* upon it, they will find, that not only a *snaffle*, but even a *ribband*, or *packthread*, will be sufficient to guide and controul the animal in all its motions. The mouth, therefore, being *made*, and without it there can be no riding, the *snaffle* will be as effectual as the bitt, and in all other particulars greatly superior to it; while it stands doubly valuable and recommended from the plainness and simplicity of its composition, and from the ease and readiness with which it may be used.

Such are the properties and merits of the *snaffle*; these, long observation and not a little experience have taught me to think preferable (generally speaking) to those of the *bitt*, and to point out and recommend, with all deference to others. Conscious, at the same time, that in doing this, I commit *high treason* against the dignity and pretended rights of the bitt, but not being legally entitled to the pre-eminence it has so long enjoyed, this sacrifice is due to justice and to truth.

——— *Detrahere ausus*

Hærentem capiti multa cum laude coronam. Hor.

---

a plank in equilibrio, and when one end is raised, the other must necessarily be depressed; elevating the head has therefore not only the effect of settling the horse upon his haunches, but of preventing numerous disorders, such as rearing, plunging, and forcing the hand.

By raising the head, or more properly speaking the neck, the elevator muscles of the scapula, inserted in the four last cervical vertebræ, act more forcibly, and that bone takes a wider angle, which enables the horse to throw out his fore legs, and raise the arms high: when that point is gained, and the shoulders well suppled in their forward motion, the head may be lowered to its proper situation.

As the primary lessons will be of very short duration, a powerful rider is recommended, that the aids may be given vigorously when occasion requires.

SECTION IX.

Of the Bridon.

The *bridon*, *martingale*, and *cavefon*, are no more than affiftants, and humble attendants of the bitt; they ought, therefore, to fhare the fate of their mafter, and fall with it. Wherever the *double-reined* fnaffle comes, it will extinguifh and banifh them from the common-wealth of horfemanfhip. In paffing condemnation, it may not, however, be improper to affign fome reafons for pronouncing fentence upon them.

The *bridon*, to be confidered in its beft light, muft be employed only as a *fecond* bridle, or *bridle* in *referve*, in cafe any failure of the firft, or *great bridle*, called the bitt, fhould call for its affiftance. In *battle*, therefore, or even in *hunting*, and upon other occafions, it may be of much fervice; for in war the reins were compofed of links of iron, and were no more than fmall chains, which could not be fevered by a ftroke of the fword, or fabre. The bridles worn by coach-horfes at prefent, when exercifed, or taken out to be watered, are of this fort, and ufed upon thefe little occafions, inftead of the bitts which they wear when put to draw the coach. The *bridons* or *fmall* bridles, are of feveral forts: fome have one *joint* in the middle, fome two, and others are quite even and fmooth. Thefe variations, however, are diftinctions which make no difference, for they all produce the fame effect. When ufed with a bitt, the *bridon* is intended fomewhat to bend the neck, but more efpecially to raife the head, and to correct the effect of the bitt in pulling it down; fo that between them, there is an eternal conteft and oppofition; but the *bridon* is not ftrong enough to ftand againft the force of its antagonift. That horfeman, therefore, who wifhes to have his horfe carry *high*, fhould ufe only a *bridon* or *fnaffle*, which is the fame fort of bridle, only thicker and ftronger; and if he would have his horfe carry his head *low*, let him employ the bitt; but to ufe them together is to endeavour to reconcile flat contradictions; inafmuch as

I

that when the head is to be *raifed* by the *bridon*, the *bitt* muſt ceaſe to act, and when the latter confines, and pulls the head *down*, the former becomes totally uſeleſs.

SECTION X.

Of the Martingale.

The *martingale*, invented by *Evangeliſta*, an eminent horſeman of *Milan*, is a long ſtrap, or thong of leather, the one end of which is faſtened to the girth, between the fore legs, and the other to the bitt, or, which is the better way, ſhould have a thin mouth-piece of its own. It is of ſervice in caſes where the horſe toſſes his head, or turns his muzzle upwards, when he *beats* upon the hand, and his head is uncertain and inconſtant; when his jaws are too tight, and when he is *ſtag-necked*. In theſe circumſtances, the *martingale*, although decried by many horſemen, will have its merit, and contribute to bring down the noſe, and ſettle the head in a juſt and, becoming poſture, till, by practice and habit, the horſe will be able to carry it with ſteadineſs and grace.

It is neverthelefs rather a rude and compulſive implement; but the faults abovementioned, being rather deſperate, require a deſperate remedy: nor is it improper to *prepare* a young and unmouthed horſe for the *bitt*, for it will confine and place the head, by a gentle reſtraint, without diſquieting and alarming the mouth at firſt, ſo much as the bitt will do; which acting, upon the *bars* and *beard*, ſubjects the horſe to greater rigour.

The difficulty in uſing the *martingale* conſiſts entirely in fixing it to a juſt meaſure, ſo as not to check the horſe, nor yet allow him in too wanton a liberty. This the horſeman muſt do for himſelf, and conſult the *make* of the horſe, his temper, and manner of going, as his guide and director.

If the *snaffle* is used with the reins fastened low, it becomes a *martingale*, or a better thing; because the hand can make it strict or easy, and *both* by turns, as the rider pleases, and the horse requires.

SECTION XI.

Of Cavesons.

This is an instrument, which, from the earliest days of modern horsemanship, even to the present time, has been employed and considered as the most effectual, and almost the *only* means of breaking and reducing a horse to suppleness and obedience. Many are the sorts which have been invented for this purpose; differing from each other in no essential point but in being of different degrees of mildness or severity; and it is astonishing to what an excess of cruelty they were carried to answer the latter purpose; they are always tied over the nose, and being made of iron, and armed with sharp teeth, harrowed and tore the poor animal in a manner that might have made a *butcher* blush, but of which the old horsemen seem to have been proud; it being a sort of proverbial boast among them, that a *bloody nose* made a *good mouth*; their chief intention being to restrain and bend the horse by the *caveson*, and to save the *mouth* at the expence of the *nose*; at the same time encumbering the horse with both, nor considering, while they thought of *saving* the mouth, that is, not making it acquainted with the *bitt*, that, till it had been properly worked and formed, it could never be true and faithful to the hand; and that in order to be *made*, it must first be prepared and seasoned; and although a raw and ignorant mouth may be spoiled by a rough and injudicious hand, yet there is no *natural* mouth, however good, that does not require to be moulded, and wrought upon by the bitt, before it can be brought to such a temper and feeling, as to act in a close and de-

licate correfpondence with the hand which is to govern it. Upon this principle, therefore, of reafoning, it muft follow, that if an horfe is to be
worked only by means of the *cavefon*, and the bitt is to be inactive, or but
flightly employed; let him be never fo well dreffed to the *cavefon*, yet,
when he comes to be rode with the bitt alone, as he ought fometimes to
be, his mouth, for want of practice, will be aukward and unformed,
though years may have been fpent to make him otherwife complete. The
cavefon, therefore, to be feen in its beft light, and allowed in its fulleft
extent of merit, fhould never be ufed but as *preparatory* to the bitt, and
as an engine to bend and fupple the horfe. In which latter office, it certainly can boaft a power much fuperior to that of the bitt, and fuch as
muft entitle it to the greateft applaufe, were it not humbled by one unhap-
py circumftance, that at the fame time that it *bends*, it *pulls down* the head,
and puts the horfe upon his *fhoulders*.

In fpite of this inconvenience, it is neverthelefs certain, that if the fer-
vices of the *fnaffle*, as abovementioned, were not known, the *cavefon* muft
ftand poffeffed of much praife; and as it is very efficacious in bending and
fuppling the horfe, may at leaft difpute precedence with the *bitt*; while
both, at the appearance of the *fnaffle*, which is *both* in *one*, and fomething
more, ought to retreat, and *hide their diminifhed heads*.

· SECTION XII.

The *chambriere* is a thong of leather about fix feet long, tied to the end of
a piece of wood like the handle of a whip, about four feet long. This inftrument ferves to roufe and animate horfes that are dull or hold back;
and to chaftife fuch as refufe to go forward. It is alfo of great ufe to drefs
a horfe in the pillars; but the proper manner of applying it muft be well
underftood.

The whip is banifhed from the general practice of well regulated fchools, becaufe too fevere; it fhould however be always at hand, as it may be required to chaftife horfes that have thick coats, and are infenfible to the application of the chambriere.

The *fwitch*, is a twig or rattan, which the rider holds in his right hand, about three feet and a half long. Were it longer, the middle would ftrike the fhoulder, but the application of the point is required, to animate without bruifing; it gives grace to the horfeman, and familiarizes him to the mode in which he muft carry his fword.

The *fpurs*, too well known to require a defcription, are ufed in the aids and chaftifements given by the legs; the neck fhould be longer than common, otherwife the rider would be obliged to give his legs too much motion when applying the rowel of the fpur.

The *longe*, is a cord, about the fize of the little finger, and twelve feet long, with knots at the intermediate diftance of every two feet, a ftrap and buckle at the end to faften to the middle ring of the iron cavefon. It is of excellent ufe, to make young horfes trot in circles, with the aid of the chambriere, and alfo in chaftifing thofe that are reftive or obftinate, by working them in circles, as will be fully defcribed in its place.*

* " Though all horfes are generally bought at an age when they have already been back-
" ed, they fhould be begun and prepared for the rider with the fame care, gentlenefs and
" caution, as if they had never been handled or backed, in order to prevent accidents which
" might elfe arife from fkittifhnefs, or other caufes: and as it is proper that they fhould be
" taught the figure of the ground they are to go upon when they are firft mounted, they
" fhould be previoufly trotted in a *longe* on circles, without any one upon them.
" The manner of doing this is as follows: Put an eafy cavefon upon the horfe's nofe, and
" make him go forwards round you, ftanding quiet and holding the *longe*; and let another
" man, if you find it neceffary, follow him with a whip. All this muft be done very gently,
" and but little at a time: for more horfes are fpoiled by overmuch work, than by any other
" treatment whatever; and that by very contrary effects: for fometimes it drives them into
" vice, madnefs and defpair, and often ftupifies and totally difpirits them.
" The firft obedience required in a horfe is going forwards; till he performs this duty

K

The *pillars*, are two round pofts, fixed upon the line that divides the area of the manege. The invention is generally afcribed to EUMENES, when befieged in the fort of Nora by ANTIGONUS, fearing his horfes fhould fall fick from want of exercife.

The height of each pillar fhould be about eight feet, and the diftance between them five, with holes oppofite to each other at every fix inches; from four to fix feet above the ground, they fhould be fo far fixed under ground as to be immoveable, and withftand the exertions of the moft unruly horfe.

" freely, never even think of making him rein back, which would inevitably make him
" reftive : as foon as he goes forwards readily, ftop and carefs him. You muft remember
" in this, and likewife in every other exercife, to ufe him to go equally well to the right and
" left ; and, when he obeys, carefs him and difmifs him immediately. If a horfe that is
" very young takes fright and ftands ftill, lead on another horfe before him, which proba-
" bly will induce him inftantly to follow. Put a fnaffle in his mouth; and when he goes
" freely, faddle him, girting him at firft very loofe. Let the cord, which you hold, be
" long and loofe ; but not fo much fo as to endanger the horfe's entangling his legs in it.
" It muft be obferved, that fmall circles, in the beginning, would conftrain the horfe too
" much, and put him upon defending himfelf. No bend muft be required at firft ; never
" fuffer him to gallop falfe ; but whenever he attempts it, ftop him without delay, and then
" fet him off afrefh. If he gallops of his own accord, and true, permit him to continue
" it ; but if he does it not voluntarily, do not demand it of him at firft. Should he
" fly and jump, fhake the cord gently upon his nofe without jerking it, and he will fall
" into his trot again. If he ftands ftill, plunges, or rears, let the man who holds the
" whip make a noife with it ; but never touch him till it be abfolutely neceffary to make
" him go on. When you change hands, ftop and carefs him, and entice him by fair means
" to come up to you ; for by prefenting yourfelf, as fome do, on a fudden before horfes,
" and frightening them to the other fide, you run a great rifk of giving them a fhynefs.
" If he keeps his head too low, fhake the *cavefon* to make him raife it ; and in whatever
" the horfe does, whether he walks, trots or gallops, let it be a conftant rule that the motion
" be determined, and really fuch as is intended, without the leaft fhuffling, pacing, or any
" other irregular gait." *Earl of Pembroke.*

CHAPTER IV.

Of the Terms of the Art.

It greatly facilitates the acquiring of any art or science to understand the terms of that art. Horsemanship has its terms, and therefore I shall endeavour to give clear and precise definitions of them.

Manege.—This word has two meanings, the place of exercise, and the exercise itself. The places of exercise are sometimes covered, and sometimes open. A covered manege, thirty-six feet broad, and thrice as long, is a good size; an open manege may be longer and wider, according to the ground, and surrounded with paling. The term, when applied to the exercise, means the manner of dressing a horse to all sorts of airs.

Air, is that graceful attitude, which a horse ought to have in his different paces; also the cadence proper to each motion he makes, whether natural or artificial, as will be more fully explained hereafter.

To *change hands,* or to *change,* is the action of the legs of a horse, when he changes his feet either to gallop with the left or the right leg foremost. This term is taken from the old masters, who named the parts of a horse from the parts of a man, in preference to those of other animals, as we still say the mouth of a horse, the chin, the arms, so they used to call the feet of a horse the hands, and the line or tread of a horse when he crosses the manege before he changes his feet, is called the change of hands.

Pist or *tread,* is the path which a horse makes with his four feet. A horse goes in one tread, or in two treads; on one tread when he goes forward in a straight line, and his hind legs follow upon the same line as the fore legs; on two treads, when he goes sideways, for then his hind legs describe one line, and his fore legs another.

This laft is called fhunning the heels, in French *fuir les talons*, in the Englifh acceptation *paffaging*.

Aids or *helps*, are the means which the rider employs to govern his horfe, and put him in motion. Thefe means confift in the different motions of the hands and legs.

Fine aids.—A horfeman is faid to have fine aids, when his motions are hardly perceptible, and when he gives the aids with fkill, eafe, and grace, preferving a proper equilibre; they are alfo called fecret aids. A horfe is faid to have fine aids, when he obeys the flighteft motions of the hand and leg of the rider readily.

To yield the hand or *give the reins*, is the motion made by lowering the bridle hand to eafe the bars, and take off the preffure of the bitt from them. It muft be obferved that the left hand of the rider is always called the bridle hand, for though the right hand is fometimes employed to pull the right rein, it is only to affift the left, which ftill retains the name of bridle hand.

To *hold the hand hard*, is the action of a rider who has a rough hand, and holds it tighter than he ought: it is the greateft fault a man on horfeback can commit, for this roughnefs of the hand fpoils the horfe's mouth, induces him to rear, and puts him in danger of falling back; a very dangerous, and fometimes fatal, accident.

To *pull hard*, is the fault of the horfe when he oppofes his mouth to the rider's hand, by raifing his nofe, and pulling, through ignorance or difobedience.

To *bear upon the hand* or *be heavy in hand*, is when the horfe fupports his head by the bitt, and is heavy upon the bridle-hand, which is in a manner obliged to carry the head.

Battre a la main, to *beat upon the hand*—this is the fault of a horfe whofe head is unfteady, and his mouth not formed; to avoid fubjection to the bitt, he fhakes the bridle, and toffes his head up and down.

Faire les forces, to *play the fhears,* or *to fhear,* is a very difagreeable trick, which fome horfes have; they open their mouths wide, and continually play the lower jaw backwards and forwards from right to left: it is the fign of a weak mouth.

Appui, ufed in Englifh with the fame meaning as in French, means that fenfation which the action of the bridle produces in the hand of the rider, and reciprocally the hand of the rider produces on the bars and beard of the horfe: horfes have no *appui,* too much, or an appui full in hand.

Thofe which have no appui fear the bitt, and cannot bear it to reft on the bars; they therefore beat upon the hand, and tofs their heads. Thofe which have too much appui, are heavy in hand: the full appui which makes the beft mouth, is fuch, that the horfe neither beats upon the hand, nor bears upon it, but has his appui firm, light and moderate; thefe are the qualities of a good mouth, and anfwer to thofe of the rider's hand, which ought to be light, gentle and firm.

A flop, the manner of ftopping a horfe at the end of his courfe or heat.

A courfe or *heat,* the repetition of a leffon, continued during a certain fpace of time, at the end of which the horfe is allowed to take breath, before he begins again.

An *half flop,* is the drawing back of the bridle-hand towards the body, to hold in, or fupport the foreparts of the horfe, when he bears upon the bitt, or when it is required to bring his head down, or to put him together.

To *bring down,* is to make the horfe lower his head and nofe, when he pulls and carries his nofe high.

To *put together*, is to make a horfe fhorten his pace or his air, and put him on his haunches; it is performed by holding him in gently with the bridle, and at the fame time driving his haunches under his body, by preffing him with the calves of the legs. It prepares the horfe to obey hand and heel.

To *be in hand and heel*, is the property of a horfe that is perfectly well dreffed, that follows the hand, and obeys the legs or fpurs, with freedom, and readinefs, either to go forward, or backward; to work on the fpot, or to either hand; to bear the legs, and even the fpurs, without traverfing, or difplacing his head: a horfe that does all this may juftly be called a *Phœnix*.

To *collect*, is to keep a horfe very much together, when he begins to be fo far advanced as to be ready to be put in hand and heel.

To *traverfe*, is to throw the croup out of that tread or line in which it ought to move, going to one fide, or ftraight forward.

S'entabler, f'acculer, to *tail*, means that the horfe, when going to one fide, pufhes his croup round in fuch a manner, that inftead of going forward, his haunches go before the fhoulders.

To *harp*, is the gate of a horfe that has a ftring-halt, and moves his hocks with a fudden jerk, inftead of bending his haunches.

To *piaffe*, is the action of a horfe that paffages or trots on the fame fpot, bending his arms and legs gracefully, without traverfing, advancing, or backing, and ftands in awe of the rider's hand and legs.

To *ftamp*.—Horfes that piaffe badly, inftead of keeping the legs high, hurry their motions as if they were beating fomething to powder, are faid to ftamp, and the fault proceeds from too much fire.

To *double* wide or large, is to turn the horfe acrofs the middle of the manege, without changing hands ; and to double narrow, is to turn round a small square at the corner of the manege.

Tride, is a word invented by Monsr. de la Broue, he used it to express that quick, short and united motion, which a horse makes when he puts his haunches under him smartly; (it may be rendered gliding in English) a horse that moves his haunches quick and short in his gallop, is said to glide, or to have a gliding career. (*Carriere Tride.*)

To *close*—applied to a demivolt or change of hands in going to one side, means bringing the four legs into the same tread, which in the Volte is a radius, or line running to the centre of the volt, and in the passage, is along the wall before he goes off to the other hand.

To *work from hand to hand*, is to turn a horse on one pist or tread, with the hand only, or with very little help of the leg: it is much used in the exercise of war.

To *help*, to press a horse forward with the houghs, or with the calves of the legs, when he wants to stop, or to slacken his pace.

To *slide* or to *slip forwards*, the action of a horse in going to one side, when the outer leg passes over the inner one. Inner, and outer, are modes of expression used instead of right, and left, in speaking of the aids given with the reins of the bridle, or with the legs, or heels of the rider; or in speaking of the motions of the horse's legs, according to the hand to which he is going: but to make this more clear, it must be understood, that horsemen formerly, most commonly worked their horses in circles; and the center, round which they turned, determined the hand to which they were going; so that in turning a horse upon a circle to the right, the rein, hand, and the leg, which were on the side of the center, were termed inner; and those further from the center, outer; in the present cafe, the left rein, hand and leg, were on the outfide, and called the outer rein, &c.

Now that maneges are made fquare, and enclofed with walls or paling, it is eafy to conceive, that the outer hand, &c. is that next the wall or paling; fo, if the left hand is neareft the wall, that is the outer hand; and the right hand, which is on the fide neareft the area of the manege, is the inner; if the wall is on the right hand of the rider, he is faid to work to the left, and the right hand, &c. is the outer hand.

I have been obliged to be a little more explicit concerning thefe terms, becaufe people are apt to confound them; but it is more intelligible and more fimple, to fay the right hand, or the left hand, in fpeaking either of the rider, of the horfe, or of the legs, or reins.

The terms which concern the airs of the manege, will be explained and defined, in the 6th Chapter, which treats of artificial motions.

CHAPTER V.

Of the different motions of the legs of a Horfe in his feveral paces.

The generality of men who ride on horfeback, have but a confufed idea of the motions of the animal in his feveral paces; and yet without this fo effential knowledge, it is impoffible for the rider to put fprings in motion, whilft he is ignorant of their mechanifm.

Horfes have two kinds of paces, the natural and the artificial; in the natural paces, the *walk*, the *trot*, and the *gallop*, are perfect; and the *amble*, the *entre-pas*, *traquenard*, or *mixed ftep*, and the *aubin* are imperfect.

The natural and perfect paces are thofe which nature teaches without any affiftance from art.

The imperfect or defective natural paces, are thofe which proceed from weaknefs natural or accidental.

The artificial paces are thofe which a fkilful mafter teaches the horfe that he dreffes, to form them for the different airs of which they are capable, and which they ought to perform, in well regulated fchools.

SECTION I.

Of the natural paces.

OF THE WALK.

The walk is the leaft raifed, the floweft, and the moft gentle of all the paces. When a horfe walks, he lifts up the legs that are tranfverfely oppofite, one before, and the other behind; for inftance, when his right leg before is up and moving forward, the left leg behind is raifed immediately after it, and follows the motion of the fore-leg; and fo on, of the other two; therefore, in the walk there are four motions, firft the right leg before, which is followed in the fecond by the left leg behind, thirdly the left leg before, followed by the right leg behind in the fourth motion; and fo on alternately.

OF THE TROT.

The motion of the horfe's legs is the fame as in the walk; the difference between thefe paces is that the motion of the trot is more violent, quicker, and higher, confequently rougher than that of the walk, which is flow

M

and low. There is alfo this difference, that though the horfe moves his legs as in the walk, yet he does it in two times only, becaufe he raifes the hind and fore-leg together, and puts them down at the fame time, but .in the walk he does it in four times, as was faid before.

OF THE GALLOP.

The gallop is the action of a horfe when he runs, and is a kind of jumping forwards; the fore-legs do not reach the ground before the hind legs are in the air, fo that there is an imperceptible inftant of time, in which all four legs are off the ground. In the gallop, there are two principal motions, the one of the right hand, which is called galloping with the right foot, or to the right; the other of the left hand, which is called galloping with the left foot, or to the left; in each of thofe motions the inner fore-leg muft go foremoft to clear the way, and the inner hind leg muft follow it, and alfo go before the outer hind leg; this is performed in the following manner; if the horfe gallops to the right, when the two fore-legs are raifed, the right leg is to be put down a little further advanced than the left, the right hind leg follows the motion of the leg before it, and is alfo put down further advanced than the left. In the gallop to the left, the left fore-leg leads the way, and is followed by the left hind leg, both are put down further advanced than the legs of the right fide; the legs take this pofition in the following order:

When the horfe gallops to the right, as foon as he has driven the fore-parts forward by the fpring of his haunches, he puts down firft the left hind leg, next the right hind leg, which makes the fecond pofition, and is advanced before the left; at the very fame time that he puts down the right hind leg, he puts down alfo the left fore-leg, fo that in putting down thofe two feet, which are tranfverfely oppofite, as in the trot, there is for the moſt part only one time that is diſtinguiſhable, either by the ſight or the ear. The right fore-leg, which is advanced before the left, upon the ſame line as the right hind leg, makes the third and laſt time. Theſe motions are repeated in every time of the gallop, and continue alternately.

To the left, the poſition of the feet is different; for in this the right hind foot makes the firſt time; the left hind foot and the right fore-foot (which two, are raiſed, and put down together acroſs, as in the trot) mark the ſecond time; the left fore-foot, which is advanced before the right, upon the ſame line as the left hind foot, makes the third time.

But when a horſe has ſtrong ſprings, and the haunches have a gliding motion, he marks four times, in the following order; galloping to the right, for inſtance, the feet are put down one after the other, firſt the left hind foot, ſecondly the right hind foot, thirdly the left fore-foot, which is put down immediately after the ſecond, and fourthly the right fore-foot: the right feet are, in this caſe alſo, further advanced than the left; and the times are diſtinctly 1, 2, 3, & 4: this forms the true cadence of the fine gallop, which ought to be performed with a briſk motion of the haunches, and to be ſhortened before, as will be explained in its place.

When a horſe, in his gallop, does not obſerve the ſame order and poſition of his feet, that has been before deſcribed, he is *falſe* and *diſunited*.

A horſe gallops *falſe*, or with the wrong feet, when in going to either hand, he uſes the outer leg to lead the way and advances it before the inner leg; that is to ſay, if in galloping to the right, he leads with his left leg before, and his right behind, he is falſe, and gallops with the wrong leg. The reaſon why he is falſe is, becauſe the fore-leg and the hind leg which are neareſt the centers, ought to be fartheſt advanced, to ſupport the weight of the horſe and rider; otherwiſe the horſe would be ſubject to fall when he turns; which ſometimes happens, and muſt be dangerous.

The fame rifk attends his galloping difunited. A horfe may be difunited in two different ways, either before, or behind; but more commonly.
the latter: he is difunited before, when in galloping to either hand, his
hind legs are in their proper pofitions for that hand, but the outer fore-leg
leads the way, inftead of the inner leg; for example, when a horfe gallops
to the right, but advances and leads with his left fore-leg, he is difunited
before; and the fame thing happens, if in galloping to the left, he advances his left leg behind as he ought, but leads with his right before. He
is difunited behind, when the outer leg behind advances before the inner
leg behind. For the better underftanding of what has been faid, it muft
be obferved, that when a horfe, in his gallop to the right, places his fore-
legs in the pofition which they ought to have to gallop to the left, he is
difunited before; and when he places his hind legs in the pofition which
they ought to have to gallop to the left, he is difunited behind: the fame
holds good for the left hand.

It is always underftood that a horfe ufed for hunting, or the road,
gallops with the proper leg, when he leads with the right leg; but
fome horfemen make their horfes change legs, to eafe the left, which is the
one that fuffers moft, becaufe it bears all the weight; whilft the right,
which only leads the way, has more liberty, and is not fo much fatigued.

SECTION II.

Of the defective paces.

OF THE AMBLE.

The *amble* is a pace much lower than the walk, but more lengthen-
ed. The horfe makes but two motions, one for each fide; fo that the

hind leg, and the fore-leg, on the fame fide, are lifted up, and put down, both together; and, in the fame time that he puts down the two legs on one fide, he raifes thofe of the other fide, and fo alternately.

A horfe that ambles well, ought to carry his haunches low, and put down his hind foot, twelve or thirteen inches before the fore-foot, this is the reafon why a horfe that ambles travels fo faft: thofe which carry their haunches high and ftiff, do not go fo faft forward, and fatigue the rider more. For ambling horfes are only fit for foft and even ground; in buggy or broken ground, a horfe cannot long endure this pace.

It is more common to fee ambling horfes in England, than in France; for the ground there is fofter, and more even; but generally fpeaking, an ambling horfe is foon worn out, and it is a fign of weaknefs in the greater part of thofe that do amble; colts ufe this pace in the fields, until they have ftrength enough to trot and gallop: a great many fine horfes, after they have ferved long, begin to amble; becaufe the fprings begin to wear out, and they are not any longer equal to the paces which before were common and natural to them.

Of the Entrepas or Traquenard.

THE FALSE AMBLE.

The *entrepas*, called alfo the *traquenard*, is a broken pace, fomething refembling the *amble*. Horfes that are weak in the loins, with ftiff fhoulders, and thofe which begin to be worn out and fpoiled, fall into this gait. Trooper's horfes, for example, which are obliged to do a great deal of work, after they have trotted for feveral years with their burthens on their backs, when they have not any longer ftrength enough to trot, acquire an irregular, quick, and fucceffive motion of the legs, which appears fomewhat like a broken amble.

N

OF THE AUBIN.

The *aubin*, is a pace in which the horse gallops with his fore-legs, and trots or ambles with his hind legs; this abominable gait is common to horses which have weak haunches, and are ruined behind, or extremely fatigued at the end of a long course; post horses, generally, instead of galloping freely, colts that have not yet strength enough to push their fore parts forward, and to accompany them with the haunches, when too much pressed to gallop, fall into this gait; so also do hunters when their hind parts are worn out, and ruined.

——

SECTION III.

Of the artificial paces:

The artificial motions are derived from the natural, and take different names, according to the cadence and posture taught those horses, which are dressed to the exercise they are fit for.

There are two kinds of exercise; the exercise of war, and that of the school.

The exercise taught a horse trained for war, is to go freely to either hand, to set off with speed, to stop, and to turn freely on his haunches, to stand fire, or the noise of drums and trumpets, the sight of standards and colours, and not to be afraid of any thing.

The school exercise, comprizes all the airs invented by the masters of the art; which ought to be practised in the school: these airs, are of two kinds; the *low airs*, and the *high airs*.

The *low airs* are those which a horse performs near the ground; the *high airs* are those which the horse performs by springing from the ground.

OF THE LOW AIRS.

The *low airs*, or thofe which the horfe performs near the ground, are the *paffage*, the *piaffe*, the *gallopade* or *fhort* gallop, the *change of hands*, the *volt*, the *demivolt*, the *paffade*, the *pirouette*, and the *terre a terre*.

OF THE PASSAGE.

The *paffage*, (from the Italian word *fpaffeggio*, which means a *walk*) is a walk, or trot, performed in meafure and time; in this motion, the horfe muft keep his legs long in the air, the one before, the other behind, croffed and oppofite as in the trot; but the motion muft be fhorter, more confined, and marked, than the common walk or trot; fo that each ftep is not to be above a foot in length, that is to fay the foot that is in the air, muft be put down about twelve inches before the foot which is upon the ground.

OF THE PIAFFE.

When a horfe trots in one fpot, without advancing, backing, or traverfing, and raifes and bends his legs high with grace, he is faid to *piaffe*. This pace, which is very noble, was much ufed in caroufals and publick fhews on horfeback; it is ftill much efteemed in Spain, and the horfes of that country, as well as the Neapolitans, are much inclined to it.

OF THE SHORT OR SCHOOL GALLOP.

The *fchool gallop* is even and fhort, in it the horfe is much together, and his haunches have a brifk motion; that is to fay, fuch as to prevent his feeming to drag them; it produces that beautiful cadence, which at once charms the fpectator, and pleafes the rider.

OF THE CHANGE OF THE HAND.

It has been faid in the preceeding chapter, that *change of hands*, is not confined to mean merely the action of a horfe when he changes his leg, but that it expreffes alfo the path which the horfe defcribes, in croffing the manege from one wall to the other, either to the right or left. In the latter fenfe, there are two things to be obferved, the one is the *counter change*, and the other, the *reverfed change*.

The *counter change* is performed, when the horfe has been carried into the middle of the manege, as if to crofs it entirely, and his head has been placed in the pofition proper for the other hand; he is carried back to the wall which he quitted, to continue his courfe to that fame hand, from which the change was about to be made.

In the *reverfed change*, the horfe is carried into the middle of the manege as before, but on his return to the wall which he had quitted, inftead of making a *counter change*, the fhoulder is turned to take the other hand; in changing from right to left, by the *counter change* he ftill continues to the right; but by the *reverfed change*, he becomes changed to the left when he reaches the wall.

The *change*, the *counter change*, and the *reverfed change*, are made either in one tread, or in two treads, according as the horfe is more or lefs obedient to the hand and heel.

OF THE VOLT.

The word *volt*, is Italian, and fignifies a *circle* or *round circular tread*. It muft be obferved that in Italy the word *volt* is confined to mean the circle a horfe defcribes when he goes in one tread; and what we call *volt* they call *radoppio*; but with us it is reftricted to mean only the courfe a horfe takes in going fideways in two treads, which are either concentrick circles, or the parallel lines of a fquare which has its corners rounded.

The *demivolt* is the half of the *volt* or a kind of half circle of two treads. Demivolts are made either in the volt itfelf, or at the extremities of a ftrait line.

There are, befides, *volts reverfed*, and *demivolts reverfed*; the *volt reverfed* is the path the horfe defcribes when he goes in two treads with the head to the center, in which cafe the fore-legs defcribe the leffer or inner circle, and the hind legs the outer or larger circle, which is the oppofite of the common volt, in which the croup is to the center.

The *demivolt reverfed*, is performed like the change reverfed; except that the horfe muft go in two treads, when the demivolt is performed. (*See Plates* 6, 20 *and* 21.)

OF THE PASSADE.

In *paffades*, the horfe is kept upon the fame ftraight line, and changes at each end of it, from right to left, and from left to right, paffing each time over the fame line.

Paffades are of two kinds; the moderate, and the furious; the moderate paffades are performed in the gentle gallop, and the horfe is kept together in a fhort and meafured cadence, both in going along the ftrait lines, and round the volt at each end. The furious paffade is performed by advancing the horfe in the gentle gallop to the middle of the line, and then pufhing off at full fpeed to the place where he is to be collected, to begin the demivolt.

OF THE PIROUETTE.

The *pirouette* is a fpecies of volt, that is performed upon the fame fpot, in a circle, the length of the horse ; the croup remains in the center, and the inner leg behind, ferves as a pivot, round which the other three legs turn. (*See Plates 6 and* 21.)

OF THE TERRE A TERRE.

The Duke of Newcaftle has very properly defined it to be a gallop in two times, and upon two treads. In this action, the horfe raifes the two fore-legs together, and puts them down together; the hind legs follow, and accompany the fore-legs, which forms a gliding and low cadence, that refembles a fucceffion of little leaps, very low near the ground, forward and fide ways; though the *terre a terre* is properly enough placed amongft the low airs, becaufe it really is performed near the ground; yet it is the foundation of all the high airs, becaufe all the leaps are generally performed in too times like the terre a terre. (*See Plate* 7.)

Of the high Airs.

All the airs that are higher from the ground than the terre a terre, are called high airs; of thefe there are feven, the *pefade*, the *mezair*, the *curvet*, the *croupade*, the *balotade*, the *capriole*, and the *ftep* and *leap*.

OF THE PESADE.

The *pefade* is an air, in which the horfe raifes his fore-parts high, ftanding in one place, without advancing; and keeping his hind legs firm upon the ground, fo that he does not mark the time with his haunches, as in all the other airs. This leffon is ufed to prepare a horfe to leap with freedom, and to give him the command of his fore-parts. (*See Plate* 8.)

OF THE MEZAIR.

Mezair means half air; it is a kind of leap, and though it is reckoned amongst the high airs, is very little higher than a terre a terre. The horse in this air, marks the time lefs, and advances more than in curvets, and it is called *mezair or half air*, becaufe it is between thefe two : it is alfo called *half curvet*, which exactly exprefies the pofition of the horfe in this action. (*See Plate* 7.)

OF THE CURVET.

The *curvet*, is a leap in which the horfe is more raifed before, marks the times more ftrongly, and is more fupported, than in the mezair ; his haunches muft accompany the fore-legs, and at the inftant thofe touch the ground, they muft mark the time in a low and gliding beat or cadence. (*See Plates* 8 *and* 22.)

OF THE CROUPADE.

The *croupade* is a leap, higher than the curvet, both before and behind : the horfe, in this air, draws in and gathers up his hind legs under his belly, and keeps them at the fame height as the fore-legs. (*See Plate* 9.)

OF THE BALOTADE.

The *balotade* is a leap, in which the horfe, when in the air, and his legs all the fame height, fhews his heels as if he were about to kick, but does not throw them out. (*See Plate* 9.)

OF THE CAPRIOLE.

The *capriole*, is the higheft, and moft compleat, of all the leaps; when the horfe is in the air, and his legs before and behind are the fame height, he throws out his heels and lafhes out with all his force, his hind legs ftrike out like a dart as if he were about to feparate them from his body.

The difference, between thefe three laft airs, is, that in the croupade, the horfe does not fhew his heels, but on the contrary draws them up under his belly. In the balotade he fhews his heels, and offers to kick without abfolutely doing fo. In the capriole he lafhes out with all his force. (*See Plate* 10.)

————

OF THE STEP AND LEAP.

This air is divided into three times. The firft is a fhort gallop or terre a terre, the fecond a curvet, and the third a capriole, and fo alternately horfes that have not ftrength enough to repeat the capriole, fall into this air of themfelves; and the beft leapers, when they begin to be worn out, do fo likewife, for eafe, and to catch the time of the leap the better.

————

Of mounting and difmounting.

Before mounting, the horfeman fhould examine with a glance of his eye the whole equipage; this attention, the bufinefs of a moment, is abfolutely neceffary, to avoid inconveniences that may happen to thofe who neglect it. See that the throat band is not too tight, which would prevent refpiration; that the nofe band is not too loofe, this fhould be buckled tight, that it may not hurt the horfe by fhifting, as well as to prevent the horfe from opening his mouth and biting. See that the mouth-piece be not fo high, as to bear upon the lips at the corner of the mouth, nor fo low as to interfere with the tufhes; fuppofing of courfe that the fhape and fize of the mouth-piece, length of the branches, and links of the curb chain, are all adapted to the formation of the mouth: fee that the latter is fo twifted, as to lie flat upon the beard, and of a juft length. See that the faddle be not too far forward, fo as to hurt the withers or impede the motion of the shoulders; and that it be near the back, so as to bring the rider and horse as near each other as possible without rubbing upon the vertebræ. See that the girths be not too slack, so as to allow the saddle to turn, or too tight; the latter is seldom a fault. See that the breast plate and crupper are of just proportion; and, if a martingale *must* be used, that the head of the horse is in its proper position, which in general is the line of the forehead perpendicular. Then let the horseman go up to the shoulder of the horse, and take hold of the reins in his right hand, to see that they lie flat, and are not twisted; from the right he takes them in his left hand, putting the little finger of the left hand between them, keeping the switch in the same hand, with the point downwards, then taking a lock of hair near the withers in the right hand, he must press it on the inside of the thumb of the left hand, and twist it once round the thumb, to prevent slipping; the reins must be kept slack, so far as not to check the horse. Let him then take the stirrup leather in his right hand, and turning it flat to the side, put his foot into the stirrup, his leg perpendicular with his knee against the stirrup leather, then let him strike the seat of the saddle with the flat of his right hand, to discover whether the horse is alarmed at the noise and motion; then taking hold of the arch or cantel of the saddle, with the aid of both hands and his foot, rise strait up, and pause for a moment before he throws his right leg over, which must be done by keeping the leg and thigh strait, from the hip to the heel, the body at the same time perfectly erect in turning.

As soon as the horseman is in his saddle, he must remove the switch into the right hand, turning the point upwards in crossing the neck of the horse; by the assistance of the right hand, let him adjust the reins to equal length in the left, keeping the little finger between to separate them, and holding them firm with the thumb upon their flat, to prevent them from slipping.

In dismounting, the same routine is observed; dropping the left hand, and at the same time putting the switch in it with the point downwards,

P

taking a lock of the mane near the withers, and putting it (as before de-scribed) into the left hand, and round the thumb. Then putting the right hand upon the pommel of the faddle, raife the body erect upon the left ftirrup, and with the right leg and thigh ftrait bring them over the croup, and clofe to the left foot, bring the right hand at the fame time from the pommel to the cantel of the faddle, paufe a moment, and defcend with the right foot, keeping the body erect, and the right hand upon the cantel of the faddle, then take the foot from the ftirrup, and the hand from the cantel of the faddle. When the rider has difmounted, let him unloofe the girths, and after moving the faddle for a moment backwards and forwards, replace it, and buckle the girths flack; then unhook the curb chain, and bringing it within the mouth, hook it fo as it may dangle loofe, pleafe the horfe, and relieve the beard, the fenfibility of which fhould be care-fully preferved.

It would be proper to accuftom the rider to mount and difmount on both fides of the horfe, as many occafions may happen to render this necef-fary. The art of vaulting fhould alfo be generally practifed.

Of the Horfeman's Seat.

The principles and rules which have hitherto been given for the horfeman's feat,* are various and even oppofite, according as they have been adopted by different mafters, and taught in different countries; al-

---

* Beginners fhould be put to ride without ftirrups, for were they allowed to ufe them be-fore they had acquired an equilibre, and were able to ftretch their legs and thighs, fo as to fit down firmly in the faddle, and clofe to it, they would either lofe their ftirrups, by not being able to keep their feet in them, or the ftirrups muft be fomewhat fhortened, to give the feet a better hold; in which cafe the rider would be pufhed upwards from the faddle, and the feat deftroyed throughout; the parts of the body, like the links of a chain, depending upon one another; fafety likewife requires that they fhould ride without them, as a fall, if a fall fhould happen, is lefs dangerous.

It is the general practice of thofe who undertake to teach the principles of horfemanfhip, when they put a fcholar upon an horfe, to mix and confound many rules and precepts together,

moſt each maſter in particular, and every nation, having certain rules and notions of their own. Let us ſee, however, if art can diſcover nothing to us that is certain and invariably true? The Italians, the Spaniards, the French, and in a word every country where riding is in repute, adopt each a poſture which is peculiar to themſelves; the foundation of their general notions is the ſame, yet each country has preſcribed particular rules for placing the man in the ſaddle. This contrariety of opinions, which have their origin more in prejudice than in truth and reality, has given riſe to many vain reaſonings and ſpeculations, each ſyſtem having its followers, as if truth was not always the ſame and unchangeable, but at liberty to aſſume various, and even oppoſite appearances. Sometimes one opinion prevailed, ſometimes another dazzled, inſomuch that thoſe who underſtand nothing of the ſubject, but yet are deſirous of informing themſelves by ſearching it to the bottom, have been loſt in doubt and perplexity.

---

which ought to be diſtinct and ſeparate; ſuch as making him attend to the guidance of the horſe, demanding an exactneſs of hand, and other particulars, which they crowd upon him, before he is able to execute or even underſtand half of them. The better way would be perhaps to proceed more ſlowly, to inſtruct more gradually, and not to think of the Aids, of the effects of the Hand, and other the more nice and eſſential parts of the art, till the ſeat is gained and confirmed.

For this purpoſe let the ſeat alone be cultivated for ſome time, and when the ſcholar is arrived to a certain degree of firmneſs and confidence, if the horſe can be truſted, let the maſter hold the longe, and the pupil, abandoning the government of him to the maſter, ride him to both hands, with his hands behind him: this will very ſoon ſettle him with firmneſs in the ſaddle, will advance his waiſt, will place his head, will ſtretch him down in the ſaddle, will teach him to lean gently to the ſide to which he turns, ſo as to unite himſelf to his horſe, and go with him; and will give that firmneſs, eaſe, and juſt poiſe of the body, which conſtitute a perfect ſeat, founded in truth and nature, and upon principles ſo certain, that whoever ſhall think fit to reduce them to practice, will find them confirmed and juſtified by it. There is likewiſe another duty too eſſential to be omitted; but hitherto I fear never performed, or thought of, by maſters otherwiſe very diligent and very capable in their profeſſion.

They never inſtruct their pupils in the principles and theory of the art, by reading lectures to them, explaining how the natural paces are performed, wherein they differ from each other, in what their perfection conſiſts, what are the elements which form the airs of the manege in all their extent, why ſome horſes ſucceed beſt in ſome, others in different, and none in all, owing to their mould, limbs, temper, and other particulars, which, by not joining theory with practice, are unknown to many who may ſhine in a manege, but work as mechanically and ſuperficially as the horſes they ride.

There is neverthelefs a fure and infallible method, by the affiftance of which it would be very eafy to overturn all thefe fyftems. But not to enter into a needlefs detail of the extravagant notions which the feat alone has given rife to, let us trace it from principles by fo much the more folid, as their authority will be fupported by the moft convincing and felf-evident reafons.

In order to fucceed in an art, where the mechanifm of the body is abfolutely neceffary, and where each part of the body has its proper functions, which are peculiar to that part, it is moft certain, that all and every part of the body, fhould be in a natural pofture. Were they in an imperfect fituation, they would want that eafe and freedom, which is infeparable from grace. As every motion which is conftrained, being falfe in itfelf, is incapable of juftnefs; it is clear that the part fo conftrained and forced, would throw the whole into diforder, becaufe each part belonging to and depending upon the whole body, and the body partaking of the conftraint of its parts, can never feel that fixed point, that juft counterpoife, and equilibre, in which alone a fine and juft execution confifts.

It is not fufficient then, in giving directions for the feat, to adhere to trivial and common rules, which may be followed or left at pleafure; we ought to weigh and examine them with fkill and judgement, in order to know how to apply them properly and fuitably, as the fhape and figure of the perfon to whom we undertake to give a feat, will allow. Many motions and attitudes, that appear eafy and natural to one man, in another are awkward and ungraceful, whence all thofe faults and difficulties, which in many perfons have been thought infuperable; whereas a little more knowledge, a little clofer attention, would convert, in the fame fubject, an awkward and difpleafing appearance, into an eafy, natural, and graceful figure, capable of attracting the eyes even of judges themfelves. Indeed, the objects to which a mafter, anxious for the advancement of his pupil, should attend, are infinite. To little purpose will it be, to keep the strictest eye upon all the parts, and limbs of his pupil's body, in vain will he endeavour to remedy all the defects and faults which are found in the posture of almost every scholar in the beginning, unless he is intimately acquainted with, and apprized of the close dependence and connection, that there is between the motions of one part of the body, with the rest, a correspondence caused by the reciprocal action of the muscles, which govern and direct them; unless therefore he is master of this secret, and has this clue to the labyrinth, he will never attain the end he proposes, particularly in his first lessons, upon which the success of the rest always depends.

These principles being premised, let us reason, and we shall display them with force and clearness.

The body of a man is divided into three parts, two of which are moveable, the other immoveable.

The first of the two moveable parts is the trunk or body down to the waist, the second is from the knees to the feet, so that the remaining immoveable part is that between the waist and the knees.

The parts then which ought to be without motion, are the fork or twist of the horseman, and his thighs; as these parts should be kept without motion, they ought to have a certain hold and center, to rest upon, which no motion that the horse can make will disturb.

This point or center is the basis of the hold, which the horseman has upon his horse, and is what is called the seat; now if the seat is nothing else but this point or center, it must follow, that not only the grace but the symmetry and true proportion of the whole attitude, depends upon those parts of the body that are immoveable.

Let the horseman then place himself upon his twist, sitting exactly in

Q

the middle of the faddle, let him fupport this pofture, in which the twift alone feems to fuftain the weight of the whole body, by moderately leaning upon his buttocks, let his thighs be turned inward, and reft flat upon the fides of the faddle, and in order to this, let the turn of the thighs proceed directly from the hips. Let him employ no force or ftrength to keep himfelf in the faddle, but truft to the weight of his body and thighs. This is the exact equilibre, in this confifts the firmnefs of the whole building, a firmnefs which beginners are not fenfible of, though it is to be acquired, and will always be attained by practice. I demand but a moderate ftrefs upon the buttocks, becaufe a man that fits full upon them, can never turn his thighs flat upon the faddle, and the thighs fhould always lie flat, becaufe the flefhy part of the thigh being infenfible, the horfeman would not otherwife be able to feel the motions of his horfe. I infift that the turn of the thigh fhould be from the hip, becaufe this turn can never be natural, but as it proceeds from the hollow of the hip-bone. I infift further that the horfeman never avail himfelf of the ftrength or help of his thighs, becaufe befides that they would then be lefs fteady, the clofer he preffed the more he would be lifted above the faddle. His buttocks and thighs, fhould always be in the middle of the faddle, and he fhould fit down full and clofe upon it.

Having thus firmly placed the immoveable parts, let us pafs on to the firft of the moveable parts, which is, as I have already obferved, the body or trunk as far as to the waift. I comprehend in the body or trunk, the head, the fhoulders, the breaft, the arms, the hands, the back, and the waift of the horfeman.

The head fhould be free, firm, and eafy, in order to be ready for all the natural motions, that the horfeman may make in turning it to one fide or the other. It fhould be firm, that is to fay ftrait, without leaning to the right or left, neither advanced nor thrown back; it fhould be eafy, becaufe if otherwife, it would occafion a ftiffnefs, and that ftiffnefs affecting the different parts of the body, efpecially the vertebræ, they would be ftiff and conftrained.

The fhoulders alone influence by their motions that of the breaft, the loins, and the waift.

The horfeman fhould prefent or advance his breaft; by that his whole figure opens and difplays itfelf; he fhould have a fmall hollow in his back, and pufh his waift forward to the pommel of the faddle, becaufe this pofition correfponds with, and unites him to all the motions of the horfe. Throwing the fhoulders back, produces all thefe effects, and gives them exactly in the degree that is requifite; whereas if we were to look for the particular pofition of each part feparately and by itfelf, without examining the connection that there is between the motions of one part with thofe of another, the horfeman would appear hollow-backed, he would force his breaft forward, and his waift towards the pommel of the faddle, he would be flung back, and muft fit upon the croup of the horfe.

The arms fhould be bent at the elbows, and the elbows fhould reft equally upon the hips; if the arms were ftraight, the confequence would be that the hands would be infinitely too low, or at much too great a diftance from the body, and if the elbows were not kept fteady, they would of confequence give an uncertainty and ficklenefs to the hand, fufficient to ruin it for ever.

It is true that the bridle-hand is that which abfolutely ought to be fteady and immoveable, and one might conclude from thence that the left elbow only ought to reft upon the hip, but grace confifts in the exact proportion and fymmetry of all the parts of the body: to have the arm on one fide raifed and advanced, and that of the other kept down and clofe to the body, would prefent an aukward difagreeable appearance.

The left hand being of an equal height with the elbow, fo that the knuckle of the little finger, and the tip of the elbow be both in a line with the hand inclined, juſt ſo that the wriſt may direct all its motions, place your right hand or the whip-hand lower and more forward than the bridle-hand. It ſhould be lower than the other hand, becauſe if it was upon a level with it, it would reſtrain or obſtruct its motions, and were it to be higher, it could not take ſo great a compaſs as the bridle-hand, which muſt always be kept over againſt the horſeman's body, it is abſolutely neceſſary therefore to keep the proportion of the elbows, that it ſhould be lower than the other.

The legs and feet make up that ſecond diviſion of what I call the moveable parts of the body.

The legs ſerve for two purpoſes, they may be uſed as aids or corrections to the animal. They ſhould be kept near the ſides of the horſe, and in a line with the man's body; for being near the part of the horſe's body where his feeling is moſt delicate, they are ready to do their office in the inſtant they are wanted.

Being an appendix of the thighs, if the thighs are in their proper place in the ſaddle, the legs will by a neceſſary conſequence, be turned juſt as they ought to be, and will infallibly give the ſame turn to the feet, becauſe the feet depend upon them, as they depend upon the thighs.

The toe ſhould be held a little higher than the heel, for the lower the toe is, the nearer the heel will be to the ſides of the horſe, and in danger of touching his flank.

Many perſons, notwithſtanding, when they raiſe their toe, bend and twiſt their ankle, as if they were lame in that part. The reaſon of this is very plain, it is becauſe they make uſe of the muſcles in their legs and thighs, whereas they ſhould employ only the joint of the foot for this purpoſe, a joint given by nature to facilitate all the motions of the foot, and to enable it to turn to the right, or left, upwards, or downwards.

Such is in ſhort the mechanical diſpoſition of all the parts of the horſeman's body! I will enlarge no farther upon a ſubject treated on already ſo amply by every writer. I have had no other deſign in this chapter, than to give an idea of the correſpondence that there is between all the parts of the body, becauſe it is only by a juſt knowledge of this mutual relation of all the different parts, that we can be enabled to preſcribe rules for giving that true and natural ſeat, which is not only the principle of juſtneſs, but likewiſe the foundation of all grace in the horſeman.*

---

* " It is neceſſary that the greateſt attention, and the ſame gentleneſs that is uſed in " teaching the horſes, be obſerved likewiſe in teaching the rider, eſpecially at the beginning. " Every method and art muſt be practiſed to create and preſerve, both in man and horſe, " all poſſible feeling and ſenſibility; contrary to the uſage of moſt riding maſters, who ſeem " induſtriouſly to labour at aboliſhing theſe principles both in the one and the other. As " ſo many eſſential points depend upon the manner in which a man is at firſt placed on horſe- " back, it ought to be conſidered and attended to with the ſtricteſt care and exactneſs.

" The abſurdity of putting a man, who perhaps has never before been upon a horſe, on " a rough trotting horſe, on which he is obliged to ſtick with all the force of his arms and " legs, is too obvious to need mentioning. This rough work, all at once, is plainly as " detrimental at firſt, as it is excellent afterwards in proper time. No man can be either well " or firmly ſeated on horſeback, unleſs he be maſter of the balance of his body, quite un- " conſtrained, with a full poſſeſſion of himſelf, and at his eaſe; none of which requiſites can " he enjoy, if his attention be otherwiſe engaged; as it muſt wholly be in a raw, unſuppled, " and unprepared lad, who is put at once upon a rough horſe; in ſuch a diſtreſsful ſtate, he is " forced to keep himſelf on at any rate, by holding to the bridle (at the expence of the ſen- " ſibility both of his own hand and the horſe's mouth), and by clinging with his legs, in " danger of his life, and to the certain deprivation of a right feeling in the horſe.

" The firſt time a man is put on horſeback, it ought to be upon a very gentle one. He " never ſhould be made to trot, till he is quite eaſy in the walk; nor gallop, till he is able to " trot properly. The ſame muſt be obſerved in regard to horſes; they ſhould never be made " to trot till they are obedient, and their mouths are well formed on a walk, nor be made " to gallop, till the ſame be effected on a trot. When he is arrived at ſuch a degree of firmneſs " in his ſeat, the more he trots, and the more he rides rough horſes, the better. This is not " only the beſt method, but alſo the eaſieſt and the ſhorteſt; by it a man is ſoon made ſuffi- " ciently an horſeman for a ſoldier: but by the other deteſtable methods that are commonly " uſed, a man inſtead of improving, contracts all ſorts of bad habits, and rides worſe and " worſe every day; the horſe too becomes daily more and more unfit for uſe. In proceeding " according to the manner propoſed, a man is rendered firm and eaſy upon the horſe, both " his own and the horſe's ſenſibility is preſerved, and each in a ſituation fit to receive and " practiſe all leſſons effectually.

" Among the various methods that are uſed of placing people on horſeback, few are di- " rected by reaſon. Before you let the man mount, teach him to know, and always to exa- " mine, if the curb be well placed, (that is, when the horſe has a bitt in his mouth, which

CHAPTER VII.

Of the Bridle-hand and its Effects.

The motions of the bridle-hand, ferve to make known to the horfe, what the rider requires; and the action of the bitt in the horfe's mouth is produced by thefe motions; a good hand ought to be light, eafy, and firm. This perfection does not proceed merely from the action of the hand, but from the rider's feat alfo, for when the body is fhaken, the rider's whole attention is employed to keep his feat; the legs too muft agree with the hand, otherwife the effect of the hand will never be juft. In terms of Art, this is called the agreement of the hand and heel, and conftitutes the perfection of the Aids.

" at firft he fhould not, but only a fnaffle, till the rider is firm in his feat, and the horfe
" alfo fomewhat taught:) likewife to know if the nofe-band be properly tight; the throat
" band loofifh; and the mouth-piece neither too high nor too low in the horfe's mouth, but
" rightly put, fo as not to wrinkle the fkin nor to hang lax; the girts drawn moderately,
" but not too tight; and the crupper and the breaft-plate properly adjufted. A very good
" and careful hand may venture on a bitt at firft, and fucceed with it full as well as by
" beginning with a fnaffle alone: only colts, indeed, it is better, in all fchools, whatfoever,
" to avoid any preffure on the bars juft at firft, which a curb, though ever fo delicately ufed,
" muft in fome degree occafion. When the bridle, &c. have been well looked to, let the man
" approach the horfe gently near the fhoulder; then taking the reins and an handful of the
" mane in his left hand, let him put his foot foftly in the left ftirrup, by pulling it towards him,
" left he touch the horfe with his toe; then raifing himfelf up, let him reft a moment on it
" with his body upright, but not ftiff; and after that, paffing his right leg clear over the
" faddle without rubbing againft any thing, let him feat himfelf gently down. He muft be
" cautious not to take the reins too fhort, for fear of making the horfe rear, run, or fall
" back, or throw up his head; but let him hold them of an equal length, neither tight nor
" flack, and with the little finger betwixt them. It is fit that horfes fhould be accuftomed
" to ftand ftill to be mounted, and not to ftir till the rider pleafes. All foldiers fhould be
" inftructed to mount and difmount equally well on both fides, which may be of great ufe in
" times of hurry and confufion. Then place the man in his faddle, with his body rather
" back, and his head held up with eafe, without ftiffnefs; feated neither forwards, nor very
" backwards; with the breaft pufhed out a little, and the lower part of the body likewife a
" little forwards, the thighs and legs turned in without conftraint, and the feet in a ftraight
" line, neither turned in nor out. By this pofition, the natural weight of the thighs has a
" proper and fufficient preffure of itfelf, and the legs are in readinefs to act when called upon;
" they muft hang down eafy and naturally; and be fo placed, as not to be wriggling about,
" touching, and tickling, the horfe's fides, but always near them in cafe they fhould be want-
" ed, as well as the heels.

The hand ought always to begin the effect, the legs to accompany it; for it is a general principle in all the paces, as well natural as artificial, that the head and shoulders of the horse must go first, and as the horse has four prin-

---

" The body must be carefully kept easy and firm, and without any rocking when in motion;
" which is a bad habit very easily contracted, especially in galloping. The left elbow must
" be gently leant against the body, a little forwards; unless it be so rested, the hand can-
" not be steady, but will always be checking and consequently have pernicious effects on
" the horse's mouth. And the hand ought to be of equal height with the elbow; if it were
" lower, it would constrain and confine the motion of the horse's shoulders; but as the mouths
" of horses are different, the place of the hand also must occasionally differ: a leaning, low,
" heavy forehand, requires a high hand; and a horse that pokes out his nose, a low one. The
" right hand arm must be placed in symmetry with the left; only let the right hand be a little
" forwarder or backwarder, higher or lower, as occasion may require, in order that both
" hands may be free; both arms must be a little bent at the elbow, to prevent stiffness.

" A soldier's right hand should be kept unemployed in riding; it carries the sword,
" which is a sufficient business for it.

" There remains one farther observation, that ought not to be omitted, about the hand,
" that it must be kept clear of the body; that is about two inches and a half forwards
" from it, with the nails turned opposite to the belly, and the wrist a little rounded with
" ease; a position not less graceful than ready for slackening, tightening, and moving
" the reins from one side to the other, as may be found necessary.

" When the men are well placed, the more rough trotting they have without stirrups
" the better; but with a strict care always, that their position be preserved very exactly.
" In all cases, great care must be taken to hinder their clinging with their legs; in short,
" no sticking by hands or legs is ever to be allowed of at any time. If the motion of the
" horse be too rough, slacken it, till the rider grows by degrees more firm; and when he
" is quite firm and easy on his horse in every kind of motion, stirrups may be given him;
" but he must never leave off trotting often without any.

" The stirrups must be neither short nor long; but of such a length, that when the
" rider, being well placed, puts his feet into them (about one-third of the length of each
" foot from the point of it,) the points may be between two and three inches higher than
" the heels. The rider must not bear upon his stirrups, but only let the natural weight of
" his legs rest on them: for if he bears upon them he would be raised above and out of
" his saddle; which he should never be, except in charging sword in hand, with the body
" inclined forwards at the very instant of attacking. Spurs may be given as soon as the
" rider is grown familiar with stirrups; or even long before, if his legs are well placed.

" A hand should always be firm, but delicate; a horse's mouth should never be surprised
" by any sudden transition of it, either from slack to tight, or from tight to slack. Every
" thing in horsemanship must be effected by degrees, but at the same time with spirit and
" resolution. That hand which, by giving and taking properly, gains its point with the
" least force, is the best; and the horse's mouth, under this same hand's directions, will
" also consequently be the best, supposing equal advantages in both from nature. This
" principle of gentleness should be observed upon all occasions in every branch of horse-
" manship. Sometimes the right hand may be necessary, upon some troublesome horses,
" to assist the left: but the seldomer this is done, the better; especially in a soldier, who
" has a sword to carry, and to make use of.

cipal methods of moving, which are forwards, backwards, to the right, and to the left, so the bridle-hand must have four different actions, yielding, reining-back, turning to the right, and to the left.

" The snaffle must on all occasions be uppermost; that is to say, the reins of it must be
" above those of the bridle, whether the snaffle or the bitt be used separately, or whether
" they be both used together. When the rider knows enough, and the horse is sufficiently
" prepared and settled to begin any work towards suppling, one rein must be shortened
" according to the side worked to; but it must never be so much shortened, as to make
" the whole strength rest on that rein alone: for, not to mention that the work would be
" false and bad, one side of the horse's mouth would by that means be always deadened;
" whereas, on the contrary, it should always be kept fresh by its own play, and by the
" help of the opposite reins acting delicately in a somewhat smaller degree of tension; the
" joint effect of which produces in a horse's mouth the proper, gentle, and easy degree of
" appui or bearing.

" A coward and a madman make alike bad riders, and are both alike discovered and
" confounded by the superior sense of the creature they are mounted upon, who is equally
" spoilt by both, though in very different ways. The coward, by suffering the animal to
" have his own way, not only confirms him in his bad habits, but creates new ones in him:
" and the madman by false and violent motions and corrections, drives the horse, through
" despair, into every bad and vicious trick that rage can suggest.

" It is very requisite in horsemanship, that the hand and legs should act in correspon-
" dence with each other in every thing; the latter always subservient and assistant to the
" former. Upon circles, in walking, trotting, or galloping, the outward leg is the only
" one to be used, and that only for a moment at a time, in order to set off the horse true,
" or put him right if he be false; and as soon as that is done, it must be taken away
" again immediately: but if the horse be lazy, or otherwise detains himself, both legs must
" be used and pressed to his sides at the same time together. The less the legs are used in
" general, the better. Very delicate good riders, with horses they have dressed themselves,
" will scarcely ever want their help. By the term outward is understood the side which
" is more remote from the center; and by inward is meant the side next to the center. In
" reining back, the rider should be careful not to use his legs, unless the horse backeth on
" his shoulders; in which case they must be both applied gently at the same time, and
" correspond with the hand. If the horse refuse to back at all, the rider's legs must be
" gently approached, till the horse lifts up a leg, as if to go forwards; at which time,
" when that leg is in the air, the rein of the same side with that leg which is lifted up,
" will easily bring that same leg backwards, and accordingly oblige the horse to back, but
" if the horse offers to rear, the legs must be instantly removed away. The inward rein
" must be tighter on circles, so that the horse may bend and look inwards; and the out-
" ward one crossed over a little towards it; and both held in the left hand.

" Let the man and horse begin on very slow motions, that they may have time to under-
" stand and reflect on what is taught them; and in proportion as the effects of the reins
" are better comprehended, and the manner of working becomes more familiar, the quick-
" ness of motion must be increased. Every rider must learn to feel, without the help of
" the eye, when a horse goes false, and remedy the fault accordingly: this is an intel-
" ligence, which nothing but practice, application, and attention, can give, in the begin-

Yielding the hand to go forwards, is a motion made by lowering the hand, and turning the nails a little downwards. In the second, or reining-back, the hand is to be drawn back towards the stomach, and the nails are to be turned a little upwards: the use of it is either to stop the horse, to make an half stop, or to make him go backwards; in this action the rider must not press very heavily on the stirrups, and when his hand makes the motion, he must throw

---

" ning on flow motion. A horse may not only gallop false, but also trot and walk false. If
" a h is gallops false, that is to say, if going to the right he leads with the left leg, or if
" going to the left he leads with the right; or in case he is disunited, that is, if he lead
" with the opposite leg behind to that which he leads with before; stop him immediately,
" and put him off again properly. The method of effecting this, is by approaching your
" outward leg, and putting your hand outwards; still keeping the inward rein the shorter,
" and the horse's head inwards, if possible: and if he should still resist, then bend and pull
" his head outwards also; but replace it again, bent properly inwards, the moment he goes
" off true. A horse is said to be disunited to the right, when going to the right, and con-
" sequently leading with the right leg before, he leads with the left behind; and is said to
" be disunited to the left, when going to the left, and consequently leading with the left
" leg before, he leads with the right behind. A horse may at the same time be both false
" and disunited; in correcting both which faults, the same method must be used. He is
" both false and disunited to the right, when in going to the right he leads with the left leg
" before, and the right behind; notwithstanding that hinder leg be with propriety more
" forward under his belly than the left, because the horse is working to the right. And
" he is false and disunited to the left, when in going to the left he leads with the right leg
" before and the left behind; notwithstanding, as above, that hinder leg be with pro-
" priety more forward under his belly than the right, because the horse is working to the
" left.
" In teaching men a right seat on horseback, the greatest attention must be given to
" prevent stiffness, and sticking by force in any manner upon any occasion: stiffness dis-
" graces every right work; and sticking serves only to throw a man (when displaced) a
" great distance from his horse by the spring he must go off with: whereas, by a proper
" equilibrating position of the body, and by the natural weight only of the thighs, he can-
" not but be firm and secure in his seat.
" As the men become more firm, and the horses more supple, it is proper to make the
" circles less; but not too much so, for fear of throwing horses forwards upon their
" shoulders.
" Some horses, when first the bitt is put into their mouths, if great care be not taken,
" will put their heads very low. With such horses, raise your right hand with the
" bridoon in it, and play at the same time with the bitt in the left hand, giving and
" taking.
" On circles, the rider must lean his body inwards; unless great attention be given to
" make him do it, he will be perpetually losing his seat outwards. It is scarce possible for
" him to be displaced, if he leans his body properly inwards."

Earl of Pembroke.

S

his fhoulders back a little, that the horfe may ftop, or go back upon his haunches.—The third effect of the hand is to turn to the right, to produce this effect the hand muft be carried to the right, with the nails turned a little upwards, that the outer or left rein may act more fpeedily, for it is the left rein which is to turn the horfe to the right.

The fourth effect is to turn to the left, the hand for this purpofe is to be carried to the left, with the nails a little downwards, to make the outer or right rein act to turn the horfe.—From what has been faid it is eafy to un-derftand, that a horfe obedient to the hand, is one that follows it through all its motions, and that the motions of the hand, produce the effect on the reins, which caufe the mouth-piece to act.

There are three ways of holding the reins, firft feparate one in each hand; fecondly, equal in the left hand; and thirdly, both in the left hand, but one fhorter than the other, according to the hand to which the horfe is to be worked.

The reins are faid to be feparated, when the left rein is held in the left hand, and the right rein in the right hand; the proper management of feparate reins is this, when the right rein is pulled, to turn to the right, the left hand muft be lowered; when the left rein is pulled to turn to the left, the right hand muft be lowered; that the horfe may know which rein he is to obey, which he could not do, if the rein oppofite the fide to which he is to turn were not lowered. The reins equal in the left hand, are ufed to guide a horfe that is obedient to the bridle-hand, either on the road, in the chace, or in war; but when a horfe is worked in the manege, to drefs him and give him a leffon, then the inner rein muft be fhortened a little in the bridle-hand, to place his head properly, to the fide to which he is to go; for a horfe that is not bent, does not appear graceful in the manege. The inner rein muft not be fhortened too much in the bridle-hand, left it give the horfe a falfe appui, and the effect of both reins muft always be felt by the hand. It is moft difficult to bend a horfe to the right, not only becaufe horfes are generally more ftiff to that hand than to the left, but on account of the fituation of the reins in the hand; becaufe the reins being feparated by the little finger, the left rein which is below that finger, acts more forcibly than the right rein which is above it; when a horfe is to be worked to the right, it is not always fufficient merely to fhorten that rein, but it is often neceffary to ufe the right rein, by pulling with the little finger of the right hand, which then performs the fame kind of office, that the left does in working to the left; very few perfons know how to ufe the right rein properly, horfemen in general lower the left hand when they draw it in, and then they only pull the end of the horfe's nofe, becaufe the outer rein does not fupport the action; therefore when the right rein is ufed, the left hand muft ftill feel the effect of the outer or left rein, that the bending may proceed from the withers, and not from the end of the nofe which is very unfeemly: It is not the fame for the left hand, the fituation of the inner rein which is beneath the little finger, gives great eafe to bend a horfe to that fide; it is to be re-marked, that when a horfe is well dreffed, the inner rein is to be but very little fhorter, and the right hand is very rarely to be ufed to bend him to the right, becaufe he ought to bend in confort with the hand and heel, but before he has acquired this degree of perfection, the reins muft neceffarily be ufed in the manner juft mentioned.

The height of the hand commonly regulates that of the horfe's head, for which reafon it muft be held higher than ufual when a horfe carries his head low to raife it, and it muft be held lower and nearer to the body than ufual, when the horfe carries his nofe high, to bring down and lower the head.

When the hand is carried forward, the curb is flackened and the effect of the bitt confequently diminifhed. This is done to pufh a horfe forward when he holds back; on the contrary when the hand is drawn back the curb is tightened, and the bitt preffes more firmly upon the bars, which is requifite when the horfe pulls on the hand: we have before faid that three qualities are neceffary to conftitute a good hand, and that it ought to be light, gentle, and firm.

The light hand does not feel the appui of the bitt on the bars : the gentle feels the effect of the bitt a little without bearing too much upon it; the firm hand holds the appui full.

It requires much art to adopt the three motions of the hand to the mouth of the horfe, fo as not to confine him too much, and not to abandon the appui at once. After yielding the hand, which is the action of the light hand, it muft be drawn in gently, to find and feel the appui of the bitt by degrees, which is what is termed having a gentle hand ; from this it is to be tightened more and more, and the horfe is to be held in a ftronger appui, until the effect of the firm hand is produced. This done it muft be again eafed, and the appui of the bitt in the hand is to be diminifhed before it paffes to the light hand, for the gentle hand muft always follow and precede the firm one ; the hand ought never to pafs from firm to light, or from light to firm at once, becaufe it would injure the mouth of the horfe, and make him tofs his head.

There are two ways of yielding the hand ; the firft, which is the moft common, is to lower the bridle-hand as we have before faid. The fecond is to take hold of the reins in the right hand above the left, and then by loofening the reins in the left hand to let the appui of the bitt pafs to the right hand, after this let go the hold of the left entirely, and lower the right hand down upon the neck ; the horfe will then be quite free, and without bridle.

This laft method is called the *defcent of the hand*, and is likewife performed by taking the end of the reins in the right hand, holding that hand as high as the head, with the arm ſtraight forward, but the rider muſt be very ſure of the horſe's mouth and obedience, before he attempts to work by this laſt method. Care muſt be taken not to yield the hand, or make the deſcent, when the horſe is on his ſhoulders; the proper time for either, is after making a half ſtop, and then when the rider feels that the horſe is upon his haunches, he muſt gently give the bridle, or make the deſcent of the hand.

This time, which muſt be taken exactly, and which it is difficult to catch, is one of the fineſt and moſt uſeful aids in horſemanſhip. As the horſe bends his haunches at the time that the appui is taken off, he muſt neceſſarily become light in hand, ſince he has no ſupport for his head.

There is another method of uſing the reins, but it is ſeldom practiſed, this is to faſten them to the arches of the banquets, by which the curb ceaſes to have its effects; this is called working with falſe reins, it is however ſometimes uſed to accuſtom young horſes to the appui of the bitt when the bridle is firſt put in their mouths. When the outer rein is uſed, by carrying the outer hand in, it carries the outer ſhoulder in, and makes the outer leg paſs over the inner one; when the inner rein is uſed, by carrying the hand out, it gives the inner ſhoulder more liberty, that is to ſay it makes the inner leg paſs over the outer one; by theſe different effects of the inner and outer rein, it is plain that the hand of the rider puts the forehand of the horſe in motion, and that he who does not underſtand the uſe of the reins of the bridle, works without rules or principles.

T

CHAPTER VIII.

Of the Aids and Instruments necessary to dress Horses.

Three of the five senses which all animals enjoy as well as man, are to be worked upon in the horse to dress him, sight, hearing, and feeling.

The sight is worked upon, when he is taught to go up to those objects that he dislikes, for there is no animal so much affected by objects that he has not seen before, as a horse.

He is dressed by the sense of the hearing, when he is accustomed to the noise of arms, drums, and other warlike sounds, when made attentive and obedient to the call of the tongue, or to the sound of the switch in the air, and to the rider's voice, which is mild and soft when used to caress; harsh and rough when it is employed to threaten him.

But feeling is the most effectual, because it is by this, that a horse is taught to obey the slightest motion of the hand and legs, by making the mouth and sides sensible if they want sensibility, or by preserving this good quality if they already possess it ; to this effect aids and chastisements are employed, aids to prevent the faults a horse may commit, and chastisements to punish him when he actually doth commit them. Since horses only obey from the fear of punishment, an aid is merely an intimation, used to inform the horse, that he will be punished if he does not obey the motion given.

––––––––––

OF AIDS.

Aids are given in various manners, viz. by the different motions of the bridle-hand, by the call of the tongue, by the whistling and touch of the switch, by the motions of the thighs, houghs and calves of the legs, by pinching with the spur, and lastly by the manner of pressing on the stirrups.

We have explained in the last Chapter the different motions of the hand and its effects, we shall therefore now proceed to the other aids.—The call of the tongue, is a sound formed by curling the tip of the tongue up to the palate of the mouth, and then suddenly drawing it down when the mouth is open; this aid serves to rouse a horse, to enliven him when he is working, and to make him attentive to the aids and chastisements which follow if he does not answer it, but it ought to be seldom used, for there is nothing so disgusting as to hear the rider continually making use of the call, besides it ceases to make an impression on the hearing which is the sense it ought to affect. This sound ought not to be loud, and should be heard only by the horse; here it is proper to remark, that a man on foot ought not to make the call when another passes him on horseback, it is a great mark of impoliteness to the rider, and is never allowable but in the case of a horse mounted to be sold.

Although the switch serves more for grace than use, yet it is sometimes employed to advantage, it is to be carried with the point upwards in the right hand, to acquire an easy manner of holding the sword.

The switch is both an aid and a chastisement, it serves for an aid when it is waved in the hand with the arm high and free, to animate the horse; when it is used to touch the horse gently with the end upon the outer shoulder to rouse him, when it is held under hand crossed under the right arm with the point above the croup at hand to animate that part, and when a man on foot touches the horse upon the breast to make him rise before, or upon the knees to make him bend his legs.

The switch is improper for horses that are to be used in war; those ought to obey the hand, to turn or bend; and the legs to go forward, on account of the fword which muſt be held in the right hand, called alſo the fword hand. The fwitch ought always to be held on the ſide oppoſite to that to which the horſe is going, becauſe it ought only to be employed to animate the outer parts.

The rider can give five kinds of aids with his legs, that is his lower parts have five motions ; that of the thighs, that of the houghs, that of the calves, that of the pinching with the ſpur, and that of preſſing the ſtirrups.

The aid of the thighs and houghs is given by cloſing the two thighs or the two houghs, to drive the horſe forwards, by cloſing the outer thigh or hough to preſs him upon the inner heel, or by cloſing the inner thigh to ſupport him if he preſſes in too much ; it is to be obſerved that horſes which are ticklifh and retain their ſtrength from vice, more readily obey the houghs when vigorouſly applied than the ſpurs, theſe in general hold back for ſome time after they are ſpurred, before they ſet off.

The aid of the calves of the legs which is given by preſſing them gently againſt the belly of the horſe, is only to put him in mind, if he has not obeyed the aids of the hams, that the ſpurs are not far off : If he fhould be attentive to this motion, it is one of the moſt graceful and moſt uſeful aids that can be given by a horſeman, to re-animate a horſe that is dreſſed, and conſequently ſenſible when he flackens the air of his exerciſe.

The pinching with the ſpurs is performed, by nicely touching the outer fkin of the belly with the ſpur, without preſſing or piercing the fkin ; this is an inſtrument ſtill ſtronger than that of the calves of the legs.

If the horſe does not anfwer any of thoſe aids, the ſpurs are to be applied vigorouſly to the belly, to puniſh him for his indocility.

The aid of preſſing on the ſtirrups is the flighteſt of all, the legs then ferve as a couoterpoiſe to keep the croup in its place, and hold the horſe as it were balanced between the heels, this aid fuppofes much obedience and fenfibility in the horfe, fince by only preffing more forcibly on one ftirrup than the other, he is determined to obey the motion; bearing on the outer ftirrup preffes the horfe and makes him go to the inner fide, bearing on the inner ftirrup fupports him and reftrains him if he preffes too much in; and bearing equally on both ftirrups, apprifes the horfe that he is to quicken his cadence when he is too flow : It is not to be fuppofed that this great fenfibility of the mouth and fides can be long preferved in horfes that are ufed in the fchools, the difference of the hands of the riders, makes them foon loofe that delicacy and juftnefs, which conftitute the merit of a well dreffed horfe; and fo delicate a fenfe of feeling grows dull in time, but if they have been dreffed upon true principles, a good horfeman will foon revive what a bad practice had deftroyed.

OF CORRECTION.

As we have already faid that the aids are only intimations given to a horfe that he will be punifhed if he does not obey thefe motions, fo the corrections are of courfe only the punifhment itfelf, which ought immediately to follow any act of difobedience to the aid that was given; but their violence muft be fuited to the temper of the horfe. It often happens that moderate correction given with judgement and in proportion, is fufficient to make a horfe quiet and obedient; while this method has the advantage of preferving the temper and courage of the horfe, of rendering the exercife more brilliant, and of prolonging the fervice of the horfe in the fchool.

Three implements are commonly ufed for giving the corrections, the chambriere or flat whip, the fwitch or fhort whip, and fpurs.

U

The chambriere, the firft inftrument of correction, is ufed to make young horfes afraid when they are trotted in the longe, and this is what they ought firft to be taught as will be fhewn hereafter. It is alfo ufed to teach a horfe to piaffe in the pillars, to drive forward fluggifh horfes that hold back and are lazy; but it is abfolutely neceffary for reftive horfes, and for thofe that are ramingue and difregard the fpur, for it is to be obferved, that it is the property of a blow given with a chambriere, applied feafonably and fmartly, to make a more lafting impreffion, and to drive a ftubborn horfe more readily forward than any correction which pricks or tickles him.

The fwitch affords two corrections, one when it is applied fmartly behind the girths, that is to fay upon the belly and the buttocks, to drive the horfe forward; the other when it is applied to give a horfe that kicks frequently, a fevere lafh over the fhoulders; this chaftifement corrects the vice more effectually than the fpurs, which he will not obey till he is afraid of them and knows them.

The fpurs are excellent to make a horfe fenfible and finely obedient to the aids; but this correction ought to be given by a man who thoroughly knows his bufinefs; they muft be ufed vigoroufly on proper occafions, but not often; fpurs applied often and unfeafonably, break a horfe's fpirit more than any thing. The fpurs muft be given about four inches behind the girths, for if they were given back (that is on the flanks) the horfe would ftop and kick, inftead of going forwards, becaufe this part is very fenfible; on the contrary, if they are given in the girths (a fault ufual with thofe who have fhort legs and turn their toes out) the correction becomes ineffectual.

To give the fpurs properly, the calves of the legs ought to be clofed gently, and the fpurs fhould follow upon the belly. Thofe who open their legs and give the fpurs at once with a kick, furprife the horfe, and he does not anfwer them fo well, as when he is firft apprifed of their approach by the clofing of the calves of the legs ; fome riders whofe legs fwing about, tickle the fkin with their fpurs continually, and this accuftoms the horfe to whifk, that is to move his tail inceffantly as he walks, which is very dif-agreeable in any horfe, but more fo in one that is dreffed.

The fpurs muft not be fharp when ufed with horfes that are reftive or ramingue, for inftead of curing one vice, they would create others ; fome horfes when they are fpurred too brifkly pifs with rage, others throw them-felves againft the wall, fome ftop entirely, and fome lie down. To accuftom fuch horfes to the fpurs, they muft be applied after the chambriere, and in the midft of the act of fetting off to either hand.

The aid of gently pinching with the fpurs, becomes alfo a correction for horfes which have very fine aids, and are fo very fenfible that it be-comes neceffary for the rider to relax entirely, and not to fit ftiff upon them, left they make ftops and plunges ; upon fuch horfes, pinching with the fpurs, how nicely foever it may be given, has the fame effect as fmart blows with the fpurs given brifkly, to horfes of a common degree of fenfibility, if not a greater.

The natural temper of the horfe muft be well known, to underftand how to make a proper ufe of the corrections, and proportion them to the fault he commits, and the manner in which he receives them ; for they muft be continued, encreafed, diminifhed, or even laid afide entirely, according to his difpofition and ftrength ; every fault a horfe commits muft not be at-tributed to vice, becaufe it more frequently proceeds from ignorance, and fometimes from weaknefs.

The aids and corrections muft be applied without making any great motion, yet much nicety and quicknefs is requifite, for the correction muft be given the very inftant after the fault is committed, otherwife they will be more dangerous than ufeful, but above all without ill humour or paffion, and always with coolnefs ; to conclude, the management of the aids and corrections may be faid to be the nicest part of horfemanfhip.

CHAPTER IX.

Of the neceffity of the Trot to make a young Horfe fupple, and of the utility of the Walk.

Monfieur de la Broue gave the moft exact definition of a well dreffed horfe, when he faid, it is that horfe which fhews fupplenefs, obedience, and regularity. If the body of a horfe be not entirely fupple and free, he cannot obey the aids of the rider with eafe and grace ; fupplenefs neceffarily produces docility, becaufe the horfe does not feel any pain in performing what is required of him, and both combined produce a regular cadenced action ; thefe three qualities are therefore effentially neceffary in what is called a finifhed horfe.

The firft of thefe qualities is only to be acquired by the trot : all fkilful mafters of the art of riding, both ancient and modern, agree in this one general opinion, and though fome amongft the latter have without any foundation, tried to reject the trot, and fubftitute a fhort walk, for the purpofe of giving a horfe fupplenefs and freedom, they deceived themfelves, for it cannot be effected, without putting all the fprings of the machine into a violent motion; by their refinement they have only lulled nature to fleep, and the obedience became foft, languid, and flow, qualities very different from that true brilliancy which is the ornament of a well dreffed horfe.

It is by the trot, which is the moſt natural pace, that a horſe is made light in hand, without ſpoiling his mouth, and that his limbs are freed from ſtiffneſs without being hurt, for in this action, which is the higheſt of all the natural paces, the body of the horſe is equally ſupported upon two legs, one before and one behind diagonally, this gives the other two, which are in the air, facility to riſe, balance, and ſtretch forward, conſequently the firſt degree of ſuppleneſs to the whole body in all its parts.

The trot is therefore the baſis of all the leſſons for making a horſe active and obedient, but though it is excellent in itſelf, it muſt not be abuſed, by trotting a horſe for years, as was formerly the practice in Italy, and ſtill is ſo in ſome countries, where horſemanſhip in other reſpects is in great repute. The reaſon is very plain, the perfection of the trot depends on the force of the limbs, this force, this natural vigour, which muſt abſolutely be preſerved, is loſt and deſtroyed by the fatigue occaſioned in a leſſon which is too violent to be long continued. The ſame effect is produced by trotting young horſes in broken and ploughed grounds; wind galls, curbs, ſpavins, and other blemiſhes of the hocks, to which horſes are liable when their nerves and tendons are ſtrained, by the imprudence of thoſe who picque themſelves on conquering a horſe in a ſhort time, but in fact it is ſpoiling, inſtead of conquering the horſe.

The longe faſtened to the caveſon, upon the noſe of the horſe, and the chambriere, are the firſt and only inſtruments to be uſed with young horſes that have not been mounted, and with thoſe that have, but commit faults, through ignorance, malice, or ſtiffneſs.

When a young horſe is firſt put to the trot in the longe, the bridle muſt not be put on, but the bridon muſt be uſed, for a bitt how gentle ſo ever it may be, would hurt the mouth, in thoſe falſe motions and ſudden ſtarts, which young horſes commonly make, before they have acquired that firſt obe-dience which is required of them.

W

I fuppofe therefore that a horfe is of age to be mounted, and that he has been made familiar enough to let men approach him, to bear the faddle, and mouth-piece; let the cavefon now be put upon his nofe, and let it be placed fo high as not to interrupt his breathing as he trots, with the muzzle fo tight as to keep the cavefon from flipping round; it muft alfo be covered with leather, to preferve the fkin of the nofe, which is very tender in young horfes.

Two perfons are neceffary for this leffon, one to hold the longe, and the other the chambriere; he that holds the longe muft be in the center, round which the horfe trots, and the other muft follow him with the chambriere, and fometimes ftrike his croup with it gently, but more frequently the ground; this correction muft be nicely managed at firft, to prevent its breaking the fpirit of a horfe that is not accuftomed to it; as foon as he fhews obedience for two or three turns to one hand, ftop, and coax him, this is done by fhortening the longe gradually, until the horfe reaches to the center, where the perfon who guides him with the longe ftands, then he who holds the chambriere, hiding it behind his back, (that the horfe may not fee it) muft go up to him, and both together muft carefs him.

After allowing him time to take breath, he muft be made to trot to the other hand, according to the fame rules and practice. As it often happens that a horfe either from too much livelinefs or for fear of the chambriere, gallops when he fhould trot, the perfon who holds the longe muft endeavour to break him of galloping, by gently fhaking the longe and hiding the chambriere, but if on the contrary, he ftops of his own accord, and refufes to trot, the chambriere muft be applied to the croup and buttocks until he goes forward, taking care however not to beat him too much, for heavy blows often repeated break a horfe's fpirit, make him vicious, give a hatred of man and the fchool, and deprive him of gentlenefs which never returns after it is once loft.

For the fame reafon alfo, the duration of the leffon muft not be too long;

long leffons fatigue and ftupify the horfe, whereas he ought to be fent back to the ftable as brifk as he left it. When the horfe begins to trot freely to either hand, and has learned to finifh his leffon in the center, he muft be taught to change hands ; for this purpofe whilft the horfe is trotting to one hand, the man who holds the longe muft go back two or three fteps, and draw in the horfe's head ; the other who holds the chambriere, muft go to the outer fhoulder and make the horfe turn to the other hand, by fhewing him the chambriere and even by ftriking him with it if he refufes to obey ; this done, let him finifh at the center, ftop him, carefs him, and fend him to the ftable.

. To make the leffon of the trot in the longe more beneficial, care muft be taken to draw in the horfe's head with the longe, and to widen his croup at the fame time with the chambriere ; this gives the longe holder greater eafe to draw in the outer fhoulder, and the circular motion which it is obliged to make in this pofture fupples the horfe.

To widen the croup is to throw it out, and to make it defcribe a greater circle than the fhoulders.

After the horfe is accuftomed to the obedience required in this firft leffon, which will happen in a few days if the method we have juft now explained be followed, let him be mounted, ufing every precaution neceffary to make him gentle in mounting. When the rider is in the faddle, he muft endeavour to teach the horfe the firft principles of the knowledge of the hand and heel, in the following manner ; let him hold the reins of the bridle feparate in each hand, and when he wants his horfe to go forwards let him lower both hands and at the fame time gently prefs the calves of his legs to the horfe's belly, (he is not to have fpurs in the beginning;) if the horfe does not anfwer the aids, which muft happen at firft, as he does not underftand them, he muft be aided with the chambriere, he has been ufed to flee from; which will ferve as a correction when the horse refuses to go forward for the rider's legs, but it must be used only at the very time the horse refuses to obey the motion of the houghs or calves.

In like manner, when a horse is to be taught to turn with the hand, the longe holder must pull in the head with the longe, at the same time as the rider pulls the inner rein of the bridon, to oblige the horse to turn if he refuses; thus the longe serves to accustom the horse to turn with the hand, as the chambriere served to teach him to go forward for the heels; in a few days he will both follow the hand and flee from the heel, if the first aids are given with that degree of judgement and discretion that ought to be used with young horses. Want of care and patience in the beginning is the source of the greater part of the vices and disorders which horses fall into.

When the horse begins to obey with readiness, and determines without hesitation, either to turn for the hand, or to go forward for the heels, or to change hands, as we suppose him to have been taught, then his temper is to be examined, that the trot may be proportioned to his disposition and powers.

Horses are in general of two dispositions, some retain their strength and are for the most part light in hand, others abandon themselves, and are commonly heavy in hand.

Those which naturally hold back, must be put to the extended full-trot to open the shoulders and supple the haunches: on the contrary those which trot heavy in hand and pull hard, must be put to the high and short-trot, to prepare them to keep themselves together; but *both* must be trained to the equal and firm trot, without dragging the haunches, and the lesson must be kept up, with the same vigour from the beginning to the end, taking care however not to let it be too long.

It muft not be the object of the firft leffons, to form the mouth, or to fettle the head of the horfe; this is not to be attempted before he is unftiffened, and has acquired the habit of turning eafily to either hand; by thefe means the fenfibility of the mouth will be preferved. The bridon is excellent in the beginning, becaufe it refts but very flightly on the bars, and not at all on the chin, which is very delicate, and the part, where the true feeling of the mouth (as the Duke of Newcaftle has very properly faid) is difcovered.

When the horfe begins to obey the hand and the legs, without the help of the longe or the chambriere; then and not before, he may be worked at liberty, that is without the longe. Let him, when he goes out of the circle, walk on one tread, to give him the line that is to teach him to walk ftraight and know the ground. When he can walk well upon the four lines, and upon the four corners of the fquare upon which he is to be worked, let him be trotted upon thefe fame lines, with the reins of the bridon ftill held feparate in the two hands; and of the four fhort heats which are fufficient each day, or each time the horfe is mounted, let two be performed in the walk, and two in the trot, and fo alternately; but let him end in the trot, becaufe it is that pace which gives the firft fupplenefs.

If the horfe continues to obey readily, in the walk and in the trot with the bridon, he may be bridled, with a bitt that has a fimple cannon and a ftraight branch.

OF THE WALK.

Although I confider the trot as the foundation of the firft degree of fupplenefs that a horfe acquires, yet I do not mean totally to exclude the walk, which alfo has its peculiar merit.

X

There are two kinds of the walk, the road walk, and the school walk. We have defined the road walk in the Chapter on the natural paces of horses, to be the least raised, and sloweft of all the natural paces, which makes it gentle and agreeable; in this pace the horse stretches his legs out, forward, and near the ground, therefore he does not shake the rider as in the other paces, in which the motions are high, and the rider is continually employed to keep his proper posture, unless he has a great deal of practice.

The school walk, is different from the road walk, because the action of it is more raised, shortened, and united.

It is of great service to form the mouth of a horse, to improve his memory, familiarize him to his rider, and render the pain of those violent lessons, which must be given to supple him, supportable; when he advances in obedience to the hand and heel, the walk confirms him in it.

But as a young horse, when he quits the trot in which he has been stretched out, cannot be at once shortened to a pace so collected as the school walk, I do not mean that he should be held in strict subjection, before he has been prepared by stops, and half stops, and which will be treated of in the next Chapter.

When a horse begins to know how to trot, the short and slow walk must be employed to give him confidence and memory; but that he may preserve the liberty of his shoulders, he must often change the line, and turn to the new one, sometimes to the right, sometimes to the left, and this new line must be either long or short, according as he retains or abandons himself.

The whole body must not be turned on the new line, but his shoulders only; and he must be made to walk forward after the turn.

This method of turning the shoulders on different straight lines to either hand, without paying any regard to the ground, but merely to turn and go forward at the rider's pleasure, is greatly better than that of working the horse on a circle, because according to this method the haunches of the horse are always in the line of the shoulders, but in the circle the horse is curved and out of the straight line. However, if the horse grows stiff again or defends himself to one hand, he must return to the circle, for it is the only remedy; I therefore recommend it as a correction, whenever the horse resists. This punishment has more effect, than all the corrections that can be given him whilst he is at liberty.

Although the lesson of working a horse upon different new straight lines, is excellent to teach him to turn with ease, yet as soon as he begins to be obedient to it, (if he is training for a riding horse) he must be walked straight forward upon a long single line, to give him an extended pace, and only be turned now and then, to preserve his obedience to the hand, and the suppleness of his shoulders. This must be done in the open country, for the ground of a manege is too confined.

If it be found that the walk is contrary to the natural temper of a sluggish heavy horse that has not been sufficiently suppled, he must be put to a brisk trot, and even corrected by the spurs or the switch, till at length he acquires a brisk and animated pace.

CHAPTER X.

Of the stop, the half stop, and the reining back.

Having demonstrated, in the preceding Chapter, that the trot is the only means of giving a young horse that suppleness which is necessary to incline him to be obedient, we must now proceed to another lesson which is not lefs ufeful, as its objeᴄt is to prepare him to put himfelf upon his haunches, and to make him pleafant and light in hand.

A horfe is faid to be upon his haunches when he finks and bends his haunches under him, and puts his hind legs, feet, and hocks, under his belly, for the purpofe of getting a natural equilibre upon his haunches, fufficient to counterbalance the fore-parts, which are the weakeſt.

From this equilibre, the pleafant feel and lightnefs of the mouth arifes. It is to be obferved, that when a horfe walks, he naturally exerts the force or his loins, haunches, and hocks, to pufh his whole body forward ; and as his fhoulders and arms are employed to fupport this aᴄtion, he is neceffarily put upon his fhoulders, and confequently heavy in hand.

The ftop, half ftop, and reining-back, are remedies, which mafters of the art of horfemanfhip have difcovered for that fault, and the means of putting a horfe upon his haunches.

OF THE STOP.

The Stop is the effeᴄt of holding back the horfe's head, and the other parts of his fore-hand with the bridle; at the fame time driving the haunches forward gently with the legs ; by this the whole body of the horfe is kept in equilibre, refting upon the hind legs and feet. This aᴄtion, which is very ufeful to make a horfe light in hand, and pleafant to the rider, is much more difficult to the horfe than turning, which is more natural.

To make the ftop well, firft animate the horfe a little, and when it is perceived he goes fafter than the cadence, help him gently with the calves of the legs ; put back the fhoulders a little, and hold the bridle tighter and tighter, till the ftop is made : when the body is thrown back, the elbows ought to be brought clofe to the fides, that the bridle-hand may be fteady; the horfe fhould keep his body ftraight in the ftop, that it may be made upon the haunches, for if one of the hind legs be out of the line of the fhoulders, he will traverfe and cannot be upon his haunches.

The advantages of a well made ftop, are to unite the ftrength of the horfe, to fecure his mouth, head, and haunches, and to make him light in hand. But in the fame degree that ftops are excellent when feafonably made, they are pernicious when made unfeafonably.

To know when to make them, the temper of the horfe muft be ftudied, for the beft leffons that ever were invented for preferving the temper will produce a contrary effect, if they are badly ufed, or put in practice unfeafonably.

When a horfe firft begins to fhew lightnefs in his trot, and eafe in turning to either hand, making ftops may commence; but feldom before this, and they muft be made by holding him in very gradually and very gently, for a ftop made brifkly and fuddenly as if in one time, would throw him upon his croup, weaken his reins, and hocks, and a young horfe not come to his ftrength might be ruined for ever. Befides young horfes, which muft never be preffed nor ftopped roughly; there are others, with which it is neceffary to ufe addrefs in making a ftop, either on account of fome defect in their make, or of fome natural weaknefs which we fhall now examine.

1ft. The head is the part that muft firft be fettled in a ftop, and if the horfe has very narrow jaws, it will be difficult for him to bear the action; if the neck is ill made and reverfed, which is called ftag necked, he will arm himfelf, and the ftop will be rough and uneven, if his feet are weak and troubled with pain, he will avoid the ftop, and be more heavy upon the hand than if the weaknefs lay in his legs, fhoulders, or haunches.

2d. Horfes that are long backed and delicate are commonly feeble in the loins, and confequently make bad ftops on account of the difficulty they encounter in collecting and putting themfelves upon their haunches, this is the caufe of feveral diforders, they either refufe to go forwards after having made a ftop, or if they do go, it is in a kind of traquenard or aubin, throwing themfelves upon the hand to avoid the pain of a new ftop.

3d. Saddle backed horfes, whofe backs are weak and funk deep, find it difficult to place their heads properly for the ftop, becaufe the ftrength of the neck depends on that of the reins, and when a horfe feels any pain in thofe parts, he fhews it by difagreeable motions of the head.

4th. Horfes that have much fenfibility are impatient, and cholerick, diflike the flighteft fubjection and confequently the ftop, their mouths are generally hard and falfe, becaufe impatience, and heat, deftroy the memory, the feeling of the mouth, and render the effect of the hand and the heels ufelefs.

5th. Laftly, fome horfes, though they are weak, ftop fhort to avoid the ftop of the rider; they are afraid of being furprifed, and will not go on afterwards; others of the fame temper, force the hand when they perceive they are going to be ftopped; both thefe kinds ought to be ftopped feldom, and when they leaft expect it. The ftop then is only proper for horfes that have ftrong reins, and ftrength enough in their haunches and hocks to bear the action: In the trot, the ftops fhould be made in one time only, with the hind legs ftraight, fo that one be not advanced before the other, and without traverfing, by which the rider will reft equally upon the two haunches; but in the gallop, in which the action is more extended than the trot, the ftop muft be made in two or three times, when the fore-legs reach the ground, that when the horfe raifes them again he may be upon his haunches, and for this purpofe when the hand is drawn back, he muft be helped gently with the calves of the legs, to make him bring his haunches under him.

Blind horfes, it is obferved, ftop more eafily than others, from the apprehenfion they are under of making a falfe ftep.

OF THE HALF STOP.

The HALF STOP is the action of drawing back the bridle-hand clofe to the body, with the nails turned up a little, not to ftop the horfe entirely but only to keep him back, and fupport the fore-parts when he bears upon the bitt, or to hold him in and to put him together : We have faid before that the ftop is only proper for a few horfes, becaufe there are but few that have ftrength enough in the loin and hocks to bear the action. It is to be obferved that the beft proof a horfe can give of his ftrength, is to ftop firm, and light, after a brifk career, which is feldom to be met with. To pafs from one extreme to the other fuddenly the horfe muft have an excellent mouth, and ftrong haunches, and as violent ftops might fpoil a horfe, or break his fpirits, they are never to be made but to try him.

This is not the cafe with the half ftop, in which the horfe is only held a little more in hand, without ftopping entirely ; this action does not caufe fuch apprehenfion as the ftop, yet it fecures his head and haunches, for which reafon it is greatly more ufeful to form his mouth, and to make him light in hand. This may be repeated frequently without interrupting his pace, and he is collected and fupported before he is obliged to fink his haunches, which is the very thing required. The half ftop is therefore proper for all horfes, yet with fome it muft be ufed with dexterity : For example, the half ftop muft never be ufed with a horfe that holds back, but when it is required to give him appui, and then to prevent his ftopping entirely he muft be helped with the calves of the legs or with the houghs, and fometimes even with the fpurs, according as he retains more or lefs ; but if he bears too hard upon the hand, the half ftop muft be made more frequently, and only with the bridle-hand without any aid of the legs ; on the contrary the thighs muſt be ſlackened, otherwiſe he will throw himſelf more upon his ſhoulders.

When a ſtop or half ſtop is made, if the horſe continues to bear upon the bitt, or to pull againſt the hand, or, as it ſometimes happens, to force the hand and to go forward in ſpite of the rider after he is ſtopped, he muſt be reined back for diſobedience.

OF THE REINING BACK.

The ſituation of the hand to make a horſe back, is the ſame as in the ſtop, and to accuſtom a horſe to go back after he is ſtopped, the bridle-hand muſt be drawn back, and the nails be turned up a little, as if to ſtop him again ; if he obeys, that is, if he goes back only one or two paces, the hand muſt be yielded, that the bars, which are affected by the ſenſation cauſed by this action, may recover their tone, otherwiſe they will be benumbed and deadened, and the horſe, inſtead of obeying and going back, will force the hand and make jerks.

Although the reining back is a correction for a horſe that is not obedient to the ſtop, it is alſo the means of preparing him to put himſelf on his haunches, of adjuſting his hind legs, of ſecuring his head, and of making him light in hand.

When a horſe goes back, one of his hind legs is always under his belly. He puſhes back his croup, and in every motion he makes, he is upon one haunch alternately, but he cannot perform this, nor ought it to be required of him, before he begins to be obedient to the ſtop and is ſuppled ; when the ſhoulders are free and open, it is more eaſy for the rider to draw the fore-part back towards him, than if they were ſtiff, and as this action gives pain to the reins and hocks the leſſon muſt be uſed but ſeldom in the beginning; when a horſe is obſtinate, and will not go back, which generally happens when a horſe has never practiſed the leſſon, a man on foot muſt ſtrike him gently with the ſwitch upon the knees and fetlocks which are the two joints of the leg, to make him bend them, at the ſame time that this is done, the rider muſt draw the bridle-hand towards him, and when the horſe obeys by going back (though it be only a ſingle pace) he muſt be coaxed and careſſed, to make him know it was the thing required from him; after the horſe has gone back a few paces with difficulty and has been careſſed for it, he muſt be kept in ſubjection to the hand, as if the rider was about to go back anew, and as ſoon as it is perceived that he lowers his haunches, and prepares to go back, he muſt be ſtopped and careſſed for doing it, becauſe he ſhews that in a ſhort time he will go back at the rider's pleaſure. To rein back properly and according to rule, every ſtep the horſe makes back, he muſt be kept ready to go forwards, for it is a great fault to rein back haſtily, it employs his ſtrength backwards in a hurry, he is in danger of throwing himſelf upon his croup, or even falling backwards, particularly if his loins are weak; he muſt alſo go back ſtraight without traverſing, that he may bend both haunches equally; when the horſe goes back with eaſe, the beſt leſſon that can be taught him is to rein back his ſhoulders only, that is to ſay, draw him back gently as if to make him go back, and as ſoon as ever he begins to do it, yield the hand and go forward a pace or two.

After a horſe has been ſtopped or reined back gently, bend his head in, by making the bitt play in his mouth, for it pleaſes the horſe, and accuſtoms him to bend his head to the hand to which he is going. This leſſon alſo prepares him for that of ſhoulder-in, which will be the ſubject of the next Chapter.

Z

CHAPTER XI.

Of the Shoulder-in.

It has been faid before that the trot is the foundation of the firft fuppleneſs and the firft obedience of a horfe, and this principle is generally received by the beft mafters; yet this fame trot, only produces in the legs and fhoulders of the horfe, a motion forwards, when he moves in one line; and a little circular with the outer leg and fhoulder when he moves in a circle; but does not teach him to crofs his legs fufficiently over, as a horfe that is well dreſſed, and is obedient to the heels to either fide, ought to do.

To make this more evident, it muft be obferved that the fhoulders and legs of a horfe have four motions. Firft the fhoulder forward when he advances in one line, fecondly the fhoulder back when he goes backwards, thirdly the motion of piaffing, when he raifes the legs and fhoulders on the fame place without moving either forwards or backwards, and fourthly the circular and crofs motion, as the legs and fhoulders ought to move when the horfe turns fhort or goes fideways: The three firft motions are eafily acquired by the trot, the ftop, and the reining back, but the laft is the moft difficult, becaufe the horfe in this action is obliged to crofs and pufh his outer leg over his inner one. If in doing this, the leg in motion be not advanced before the other, or carried round it by a circular motion, he will ftrike it againft that which fupports him, and the pain of the ftroke may either lame him or caufe him to take a falfe pofition, this often happens to horfes which are not fufficiently fupple in their fhoulders.

The difficulty of eftablifhing a mode by which this circular motion of the legs and fhoulders may be acquired with eafe, has given horfemen much trouble, becaufe a horfe which is not perfect in it, cannot turn readily or go fideways gracefully.

That we may more fully underſtand this leſſon of the ſhoulder-in, the moſt difficult and moſt uſeful of all that are practiſed to ſupple horſes, let us examine what Monſieur de la Broue and the Duke of Newcaſtle ſay on the ſubject of the circle, which according to the latter, is the only means of ſuppling a horſe's ſhoulders.

Monſieur de la Broue ſays, " the tempers and diſpoſitions of all horſes are " not ſuited to the extraordinary ſubjection neceſſary to make them ſupple " by turning continually in circles, and their ſtrength being inſufficient to " enable them to make many revolutions at one time, they become diſheart- " ened and grow ſtiff inſtead of ſupple."

The Duke of Newcaſtle ſays, " the head in and the croup out in a circle " puts the horſe upon the ſhoulders, he takes the appui and his ſhoulders " become ſupple.

" When a horſe gallops or trots with his head in and his croup out, his " fore-parts are forced towards the center and the croup is thrown out, be- " cauſe he is more confined in the ſhoulder than in his hind parts: The " parts which paſs over the great circle work moſt, becauſe they move " faſter than the parts which go on the little circle, they have a greater " ſpace to move through and the legs muſt be more at liberty; the parts " that are in the little circle are more conſtrained and ſubjected, becauſe " they bear the whole weight of the body, and becauſe thoſe which are " in the great circle are longer off the ground. The ſhoulder cannot " be ſuppled unleſs the inner leg behind be advanced before and cloſe to " the outer leg behind, as the horſe works."

From their own words therefore it appears that both theſe great men made uſe of the circle, but Mons. de la Broue ſometimes gave the ſquare the preference.

The Duke of Newcaſtle acknowledges the inconvenience of the circle (though it was his favourite leſſon) when he ſays that in the circle with the head to the center and the croup out, the fore-parts are more confined and conſtrained than the hind parts, and that it puts the horſe upon his ſhoulders.

This acknowledgement which is confirmed by experience, proves clearly that the circle is not the true means to ſupple the ſhoulders perfectly, becauſe any part that is conſtrained and loaded by its own weight cannot become light; and beſides it is very true as this illuſtrious author admits, that the ſhoulder cannot be made ſupple unleſs the inner hind leg be kept near to, and advanced before, the outer hind leg, in the action of the walk. It was this judicious remark that ſet me upon inventing this leſſon of the ſhoulder-in which is about to be explained.

When a horſe has learned to trot freely to either hand, in the circle, or on a ſtraight line; when he can walk in them with a ſteady equal pace, and has been accuſtomed to make ſtops, and half ſtops, and turn his head in; walk him along the line in a ſlow and ſhort ſtep, and place him ſo that his haunches may deſcribe one line and his ſhoulders another: Let the line of the haunches be cloſe to the wall, that of the ſhoulders about a foot and half or two feet from it, and bend his head to the hand to which he is going; which means, that inſtead of keeping the horſe ſtraight from the ſhoulders to the haunches upon the line along the ſide of the wall, his head and ſhoulders muſt be turned a little in towards the center of the manege, as if he was about to turn entirely, and whilſt he is in this oblique and circular attitude, walk him forwards along the ſide of the wall, aiding with the inner rein and leg; he cannot do this in ſuch an attitude, without croſſing and putting the inner fore-leg over the outer one, and the hinder inner leg over the outer leg, as it is eaſy to perceive in the figure of the ſhoulder-in given in the beginning of this Chapter, and the ground plan of the leſſon which more fully explains it.

This leſſon produces ſo many and ſuch good effects, that I conſider it as the firſt and the laſt of all leſſons to make a horſe perfectly ſupple and free in every part; and this is ſo true, that if a horſe which has been once made ſupple by this principle, and afterwards ill managed either in the ſchool or from ignorance, be put to it again by a horſeman, he will in a few days be as ſupple and as eaſy as he was at firſt. In the firſt place this leſſon ſupples the ſhoulders, becauſe, the inner fore-leg croſſes and is puſhed forward over the outer one, in every ſtep the horſe takes whilſt he is in this atti‑ tude; and as the inner foot is put down beyond, and upon the ſame line as the outer one, the exertion which the horſe is obliged to make in this action, neceſſarily forces the muſcles of thoſe parts into motion.

2. The ſhoulder in prepares a horſe to put himſelf upon his haunches, becauſe, in every ſtep he takes in this poſture, he carries his inner hind leg forward under his belly, and puts it down beyond the outer one, which he cannot do without bending his haunches; he is therefore upon one haunch when he goes to one hand, and upon the other haunch when he goes to the other hand, conſequently learns to bend his ſtiffle and hocks under him, which is termed being on the haunches.

3. This leſſon teaches a horſe obedience to the heels, becauſe in every motion he makes, as he is obliged to carry his legs over each other both be‑ fore and behind, he acquires by ſo doing a facility of putting forwards his legs to either hand, which he muſt perform to go freely ſideways. When a horſe is walked ſhoulder in to the right, he is prepared to obey the heels to go to the left, becauſe the right ſhoulder is ſuppled in this poſture; and when he is walked ſhoulder in to the left, the left ſhoulder is ſuppled, and he is taught to paſs his left leg to go freely ſideways to the right.

To change hands in this leſſon of the ſhoulder-in, ſuppoſe from right to left; keep the head and neck bent, and as ſoon as the horſe quits the wall, walk him with his ſhoulders and haunches ſtraight, upon one oblique line

A a

until he reaches the oppofite wall; then carry him to the wall, turn his head to the left with his fhoulder in, keep the fore-parts at a diftance from the line of the wall, and make him crofs the inner legs to this hand over the outer ones, as has been explained above for the right hand.

As the horfe will fail in the execution of the firft leffons of fhoulder-in, and will either throw in his croup, turn his fhoulders too much in, or quit the line of the wall, to avoid the neceffity of paffing and croffing his legs in a pofture which keeps every mufcle contracted (which is a great conftraint till he is ufed to it) the circle muft be ufed to correct thefe defences.

Walk him therefore in a large circle, and get from him at times a few paces, in which the inner legs are croffed over the outer ones; enlarge the circle by degrees, till he is brought as it were infenfibly to the line of the wall, in the attitude of fhoulder in, and make him walk a few paces forward, along the wall, then ftop him, bend his head and neck by fhaking the bitt in his mouth by means of the inner rein, carefs him, and fend him away.

If a horfe holds back and defends himfelf through obftinacy, and will not fubmit to the fubjection which this leffon requires; it muft be dropped for fome time, and he muft be put to the extended and free trot, both in ftraight lines and circles; as foon as he becomes obedient, refume the leffon of fhoulder in, along the wall; and if he goes well a few paces, ftop him, carefs him, and difmount.

As foon as the horfe begins to go well fhoulder in to either hand, he muft be taught to take the corners, which is the moft difficult part of the leffon.

To do this at every corner, that is at the end of every ftraight line, make him carry his fhoulders into the corner, but keep his head in the attitude of fhoulder in, and at the time his fhoulders are turned on the new line, make him carry his haunches in their turn into that corner, out of which his shoulders paffed: The horfe is carried forwards into the corner by the inner rein and inner leg; but when he is to be turned upon the new line, it is to be done by the outer rein, carrying the hand in, at the inftant the inner leg is up and about to be put down, that by turning the hand at this inftant, the outer fhoulder may pafs before the inner one; the aid requifite to turn is a kind of half ftop, and when the hand is carried in, he muft be gently preffed with the calves of both legs, to drive him a little forwards. If the horfe refufes to carry his croup into the corner, by widening his hinder parts or ftiffening his inner legs, (which is a very common defence) punifh him a little with the inner fpur, at the time that his fhoulders are turned upon the new line.

This is what I call *taking the corner*, and not what horfemen generally fuppofe it, who commonly are contented with carrying the fhoulder into the corner, and neglect to make the croup follow it; fo that the horfe turns *entier*; whereas by making the croup follow the fhoulders, not only thofe parts are fuppled, but the fides alfo, which greatly augments the force of the fprings of the other parts of the body.

By examining the mechanifm and ftructure of a horfe, the utility of the fhoulder in may eafily be conceived, and it muft be allowed (for the reafons which I have given) that the principle has nature for its foundation, which never deceives when not conftrained beyond due bounds: If the action of the legs of a horfe moving in a circle, with the head and croup out, be attended to, it will be perceived that the haunches only acquire that fuppling, which it is pretended is given to the fhoulders by the circle, for it is certain that the parts which have the greater motion are the moft fuppled. I therefore admit the circle to give the horfe the firft fupplenefs, and alfo to chaftife and break thofe of their obftinacy that refift by carrying in the croup in defiance of the rider; but I neverthelefs confider the leffon of fhoulder in as indifpenfably neceſſary to compleat the ſuppleneſs of the ſhoulders, and to give a horſe that facility of paſſing the legs which is a degree of perfection all horſes ſaid to be well broken and well dreſſed ought to acquire. *

* " When a horſe is well prepared and ſettled in all his motions, and the rider firm, it will " be proper then to proceed on towards a farther ſuppling and teaching of both.

" In ſetting out upon this new work, begin by bringing the horſe's head a little more " inwards than before, pulling the inward rein gently to you by degrees. When this is " done, try to gain a little on the ſhoulders, by keeping the inward rein the ſhorter, as " before, and the outward one croſſed over towards the inward one. The intention of " theſe operations is this : The inward rein ſerves to bring in the head, and procures the " bend ; whilſt the outward one, that is a little croſſed, tends to make that bend perpendi- " cular, and as it ſhould be, that is to ſay, to reduce the noſe and the forehead to be in a " perpendicular line with each other : it alſo ſerves, if put forwards, as well as alſo croſſed, " to put the horſe forwards, if found neceſſary ; which is often requiſite, many horſes being " apt in this and other works rather to loſe their ground backwards than otherwiſe, when " they ſhould rather advance ; if the noſe were drawn in towards the breaſt, beyond the " perpendicular, it would confine the motion of the ſhoulders, and have other bad effects. " All other bends, beſides what are above ſpecified, are falſe. The outward rein, being " croſſed, not in a forward ſenſe, but rather a little backwards, ſerves alſo to prevent the " outward ſhoulder from getting too forwards, and makes it approach the inward one ; " which facilitates the inward leg's croſſing over the outward one, which is the motion that " ſo admirably ſupples the ſhoulders. Care muſt be taken, that the inward leg paſs over the " outward one, without touching it : this inward leg's croſſing over muſt be helped alſo by " the inward rein, which you muſt croſs towards and over the outward rein, every time the " outward leg comes to the ground, in order to lift and help the inward leg over " it : at any other time, but juſt when the outward leg comes to the ground, it " would be wrong to croſs the inward rein, or to attempt to lift up the inward leg " by it ; nay, it would be demanding an abſolute impoſſibility, and lugging about " the reins and horſe to no purpoſe : becauſe in this caſe, a very great part of the " horſe's weight reſting then upon that leg, would render ſuch an attempt not only fruit- " leſs, but alſo prejudicial to the ſenſibility of the mouth, and probably oblige him to defend " himſelf ; and, moreover, it would put the horſe under a neceſſity of ſtraddling before, " and alſo of leading with the wrong leg, without being productive of any ſuppling motion " whatſoever.

" When the horſe is thus far familiarly accuſtomed to what you have required of him, " then proceed to effect by degrees the ſame croſſing in his hinder legs.

" By bringing in the fore legs more, you will of courſe engage the hinder ones in the " ſame work : if they reſiſt, the rider muſt bring both reins more inward ; and, if neceſſary, " put back alſo, and approach his inward leg to the horſe ; and if the horſe throws out his " croup too far, the rider muſt bring both reins outwards, and, if abſolutely neceſſary, he " muſt alſo make uſe of his outward leg, in order to replace the horſe properly : obſerving " that the croup ſhould always be conſiderably behind the ſhoulders, which in all actions " muſt go firſt ; and the moment that the horſe obeys, the rider muſt put his hand and leg " again in their uſual poſition.

" Nothing is more ungraceful in itſelf, more detrimental to a man's ſeat, or more deſtruc- " tive of the ſenſibility of a horſe's ſides, than a continual wriggling unſettledneſs in a " horſeman's legs, which prevents the horſe from ever going a moment together true, ſteady, " or determined.

CHAPTER XII.

Of the Croup to the Wall.

Thofe that put the head of the horfe to the wall to teach him to go to one fide, make a great miftake, as it is eafy to demonftrate. This method rather makes him work mechanically than in obedience to the hand and heels; when he is removed from the wall, and an attempt is made to make him go to one fide in the middle of the manege, having no object in view,

"A horfe fhould never be turned, without firft moving a ftep forwards: and when it is " doing, the rider muft not lift his elbow, and difplace himfelf; a motion only of the " hand from the one fide to the other being fufficient for that purpofe. It muft alfo be a " conftant rule, never to fuffer a horfe to be ftopped, mounted, or difmounted, but when " he is well placed. The flower the motions are, when a man or horfe is taught any " thing, the better.

"At firft the figures worked upon muft be great, and afterwards made lefs by degrees, " according to the improvement, which the man and horfe make; and the cadenced pace " alfo, which they work in, muft be accordingly augmented. The changes from one fide " to the other muft be in a bold determined trot, and at firft quite ftraight forwards, " without demanding any fide motion on two piftes, which is very neceffary to require " afterwards when the horfe is fufficiently fuppled. By two piftes is meant, when the fore- " parts and hinder parts do not follow, but defcribe two different lines.

"In the beginning, a longe is ufeful on circles, and alfo on ftraight lines, to help both " the rider and the horfe; but afterwards, when they are grown more intelligent, they " fhould go alone. At the end of the leffon, rein back; then put the horfe, by a little " at a time, forwards, by approaching both legs gently to his fides, and playing with the " bridle: if he rears, pufh him out immediately into a full trot. Shaking the cavefon on " the horfe's nofe, and alfo putting one's felf before him and rather near to him, will " generally make him back, though he otherwife refufe to do it: and moreover a flight ufe " and approaching of the rider's legs, will fometimes be neceffary in backing, in order to pre- " vent the horfe from doing it too much upon his fhoulders; but the preffure of the legs " ought to be very fmall, and taken quite away the moment that he puts himfelf enough " upon his haunches. If the horfe does not back upon a ftraight line properly, the rider " muft not be permitted to have recourfe immediately to his leg, and fo diftort himfelf by " it; but firft try, if croffing over his hand and reins to which ever fide may be necef- " fary, it will not be alone fufficient: which moft frequently it will; if not, then employ " the leg.

"After a horfe is well prepared and fettled, and goes freely on in all his feveral paces, " he ought to be in all his works kept, to a proper degree, upon his haunches, with his " hinder legs well placed under him; whereby he will be always pleafant to himfelf and his " rider, will be light in hand, and ready to execute whatever may be demanded of him, " with facility, vigour, and quicknefs.

B b

he obeys the hand and heels but very imperfectly, though they are the only guides that ought to be used to conduct the horse in all his paces. Another disorder takes its rise from this practice, instead of passing the outer leg over the inner one, he often passes it under, for fear of striking the leg that is upon the ground with the shoe of the foot in motion, and for fear of hitting his knees against the wall, when he raises his leg to carry it forward and pass it over the other. Monsieur de la Broue is of this opinion, for he forbids the use of the wall to teach a horse to go to one side unless he be heavy in hand, and so far is he from recommending this lesson, that he expressly says the horse then must be two paces from the wall, so that his head would be at about four feet distance.

I therefore cannot conceive why horsemen place a horse with his head to the wall, and then force him to go sideways by means of the leg, the spur, and even the chambriere held by a man on foot; it seems to me much more reasonable to avoid all this embarrassment, and the disorders which arise from it, by placing the croup to the wall; a lesson derived from that of the shoulder in.

" The common method that is used of forcing a horse sidewise, is a most glaring absur-
" dity, and very hurtful to the animal in its consequences; for instead of suppling him, it
" obliges him to stiffen and defend himself, and often makes a creature that is naturally
" benevolent, restive, frightened, and vicious.

" For horses, who have very long and high fore-hands, and who poke out their noses,
" a running snaffle is of excellent use; but for such as bore and keep their heads low, a
" common one is preferable; though any horse's head indeed may be kept up also with a
" running one, by the rider's keeping his hands very high and forwards: but whenever
" either is used alone without a bridle upon horses that carry their heads low and that bore,
" it must be sawed about from one side to the other.

" This lesson of the *epaule en dedans* should be taught to such people as are likely to become
" useful in helping to teach men and to break horses; and the more of such that can be
" found the better: none others should ever be suffered upon any occasion to let their
" horses look any way besides the way they are going. But all horses whatever, as likewise
" all men who are designed for the teaching of others, must go thoroughly and perfectly
" through this excellent lesson, under the directions of intelligent instructors, and often prac-
" tise it too afterwards; and when that is done, proceed to and be finished by the lessons
" of head and tail to the wall."

Earl of Pembroke.

We have already said in the preceding Chapter, that by working a horse shoulder in to the right, the right shoulder is suppled; that the right leg acquires a facility of stepping over the left when he goes to the left; and that, in the like manner, by working shoulder in to the left, the left shoulder is made supple, and prepared to pass freely over the right, in going to the right; according to this principle, which is incontestible, it is very easy to change the lesson of shoulder in, to that of croup to the wall in the manner following.

When a horse is obedient to both hands in the lesson of shoulder in, and consequently passes the inner leg over the outer leg freely, for example, when working to the right, as soon as he has turned a corner to the end of the manege, stop him there with the croup opposite to, and about two feet distance from the wall, that he may not rub his tail against it. Then instead of going forward shoulder in, hold him back with the hand, and press him with the left leg, to get him a few steps to the right, if he obeys only for two or three steps, stop, and caress him, that he may know this is what was required.

As the novelty of this lesson embarrasses a horse when it is first put in practice, he must be worked very gently in the beginning, with the reins separate, that the shoulders may the more easily be held back, and it must not be attempted to bend him, but merely to make him go sideways without attending to niceties; as soon as he goes to one side two or three paces without hesitation, stop for a short time, caress him, and then set out again sideways. Thus, continue to stop, and caress him, for every little mark of obedience, and then again set out, till the horse arrives in this posture at the other end of the line or wall, and in the other corner. Let him now rest a little in the place where he finished, and then return sideways to the left upon the same line, making use of the right leg to go to the left, stopping and caressing him after every two or three steps that he makes perfectly and readily, till he reaches that corner from which he first set out.

If a horfe abfolutely refufes to go to one of the fides, it is a proof that he has not been fufficiently fuppled to the other: in this cafe put him to the fhoulder in, to the fide oppofite to that to which he refufed to go. For example, if the horfe refufes to go to the right, with the croup to the wall, on being preffed with the left leg, which is the aid that ought to be given to go to the right, put him to the fhoulder in to the left, until he can pafs his left leg with eafe over the right; and that he may be brought, without perceiving it, to go with the croup to the wall to the right, which we fuppofe the fide to which he refufed to go, turn in his head and fhoulders more and more till they are oppofite to the croup, then place his head ftraight, and keep him going on from the left heel, as if he were going fhoulder in, and he will go to the right. If the horfe refufes to go to the left, work him fhoulder in to the right, infenfibly turn his fhoulders very much in, till they are oppofite to the croup, and he will be brought to go to the left.

From what has been faid, it is evident that what is called fhoulder in to one hand, becomes fhoulder out when the croup is to the wall, becaufe the fame fhoulder continues its motion, though the horfe goes to the other hand, but becaufe the pofture of the horfe that goes to one fide with his croup to the wall, ought to be almoft ftraight from the fhoulders to the haunches, the action of the fhoulder is more circular, and the motion more painful and difficult for the horfe to perform than that of fhoulder in. A little attention will make this difference evident, and fully prove that one of the advantages of fhoulder in is, that it teaches a horfe to pafs and flip one leg freely and clearly over the other, and that it is a remedy for all the faults he may commit in learning to go to one fide. When a horfe begins to go to one fide freely to either hand with the croup to the wall, he muft be put into the pofture he ought to have to obey the heel gracefully, which depends on the due obfervance of three effential points.

The firft is to make the fhoulders go before the haunches, for otherwife

the circular motion of the outer leg and fhoulder which fhews the grace and fupplenefs of thofe parts would be loft; at leaft, half the fhoulders ought to go before the haunches, (fuppofe for example the horfe is going to the right) then the pofition of the right foot behind muft be on the fame line as the left foot before; * for if the croup goes before the fhoulders the horfe becomes awry, the inner leg behind goes before and is put down farther forward than the fore-leg of the fame fide, which makes the horfe wide behind and of courfe upon his hocks, for to be upon the haunches he muft be narrow behind when he moves.

The fecond object of attention ought to be, to bend the horfe to the hand to which he goes, as foon as he begins to go freely to either hand with the croup to the wall. A bend gives the horfe grace, brings his outer fhoulder into its proper place, and makes the motion of it free and forward. To accuftom him to bend to the fide to which he goes, when ftopped at the end of the line in going croup to the wall, pull his head round with the inner rein, by playing the bitt in his mouth, and as foon as he yields to this motion, carefs him with the hand of that fide to which he bends his head, do the fame with the other hand at the clofe of the leffon to that hand, and thus by degrees the horfe will acquire a habit of going bent, and of looking to his ground in going to one fide.

The third thing to be obferved is, to make the horfe defcribe two lines or treads (that is the line of his fhoulders, and the line of his haunches) parallel, without advancing, or backing. As this in a great meafure depends on the natural difpofition of the horfe, it generally happens that a horfe which is full in hand quits the line by going forward. He muft be kept back with the bridle-hand without aiding with the legs. On the contrary thofe which have the vile trick of retaining or running back againft the wall, muft be driven forwards with the houghs, the calves, and even the

---

* Vide Plate 14.

C c

spurs, according as they retain lefs or more, by thefe precautions both kinds may be kept in order and obedience to the hand and heel.

Left a horfe in going to one fide fhould fall into a habit of traverfing or of throwing himfelf upon one leg or the other in defiance of the rider, let him be carried ftraight between the heels, upon one tread, and on the line of the middle of the manege at the end of every courfe, there he muft be taught alfo to go back, ftraight and balanced between the heels.

Although the leffons of fhoulder-in and croup to the wall, which ought to be infeparable, are excellent to give a horfe that fupplenefs, bend, and beautiful pofture in which he ought to move, to walk with grace and lightnefs, yet the leffon of the trot on ftraight lines and circles is not to be entirely abandoned. Thefe are the firft principles, and muft be reverted to, to give the horfe bold action, fupported equally by the fhoulders and the haunches, and to confirm him in it. By thefe means the horfe is divefted and eafed from the fubjection which he muft be kept in when he is in the attitude of the fhoulder in or croup to the wall, therefore to make thefe leffons beneficial obferve the following courfe.

Make three fhort courfes daily, and divide each into three parts, which is fufficient for a horfe advanced far enough to perform what we have def-cribed in this Chapter. Let the firft courfe be fhoulder-in, and after the change of hands made on one tread (for at firft he muft not go on two treads in the change) put him with his croup to the wall to both hands, and end ftraight in the walk of one tread in the middle of the manege. Let the fecond courfe be the bold and high trot of one tread, and end in the fame place upon the line of the middle of the manege without putting him to the croup to the wall.

In the laft courfe he muft be put to the fhoulder-in in the walk, then the croup to the wall, and always end in the middle of the manege. By thus mixing the three leffons of the fhoulder-in, croup to the wall, and the trot,

the horſe will be perceived daily to come forward, and to encreaſe in ſuppleneſs and obedience, which as we have before ſaid are the two firſt qualities of a dreſſed horſe.*

" * This leſſon ſhould be practiſed immediately after that of the *epaule en dedans*, in
" order to place the horſe properly the way he goes, &c. The difference between the
" head to the wall and the croup to the wall, conſiſts in this : in the former, the fore-parts
" are more remote from the centre, and go over more ground ; in the latter, the hinder
" parts are more remote from the centre, and conſequently go over more ground : in both,
" as likewiſe in all other leſſons, the ſhoulders muſt go firſt. In riding horſes, the head to
" the wall is the eaſier leſſon of the two at firſt, the line to be worked upon being marked
" by the wall, not far from his head.

" The motion of the legs to the right, is the ſame as that of the *epaule en dedans* to the
" left, and ſo *vice verſa* ; but the head is always bent and turned differently : in the
" *epaule en dedans*, the horſe looks the contrary way to that which he goes ; in this, he looks
" the way he is going.

" In the beginning, very little bend muſt be required ; too much at once would aſtoniſh
" the horſe, and make him defend himſelf : it is to be augmented by degrees. If the horſe
" abſolutely refuſes to obey, it is a ſign that either he or his rider has not been ſufficiently
" prepared by previous leſſons. It may happen, that weakneſs or a hurt in ſome parts
" of the body, or ſometimes temper, though ſeldom, may be the cauſe of the horſe's
" defending himſelf : it is the rider's buſineſs to find out from whence the obſtacle ariſes ; and
" if he finds it to be from the firſt mentioned cauſe, the previous leſſons muſt be reſumed
" again for ſome time ; if from the ſecond, proper remedies muſt be applied ; and if from
" the laſt cauſe, when all fair means that can be tried have failed, proper corrections with
" coolneſs and judgement muſt be uſed.

" In practiſing this leſſon to the right, bend the horſe to the right with the right rein ;
" helping the left leg over the right (at the time when the right leg is juſt come to the
" ground), with the left rein croſſed towards the right, and keeping the right ſhoulder
" back with the right rein towards your body, in order to facilitate the left leg's croſſing
" over the right ; and ſo likewiſe *vice verſa* to the left, each rein helping the other by their
" properly mixed effects. In working to the right, the rider's left leg helps the hinder parts
" on to the right, and his right leg ſtops them if they get too forwards ; and ſo *vice verſa*
" to the left : but neither ought to be uſed, till the hand being employed in a proper man-
" ner has failed, or finds that a greater force is neceſſary to bring about what is required
" than it can effect alone : for the legs ſhould not only be correſponding with, but alſo ſubſer-
" vient to, the hand ; and all unneceſſary aids, as well as all force, ought always to be
" avoided as much as poſſible.

" In the execution of all leſſons, the equilibre of the rider's body is of great uſe to the
" horſe : it ought always to go with and accompany every motion of the animal ; when
" to the right, to the right ; and when to the left, to the left.

" Upon all horſes, in every leſſon and action, it muſt be obſerved, that there is no horſe
" but has his own peculiar appui or degree of bearing, and alſo a ſenſibility of mouth, as
" likewiſe a rate of his own, which it is abſolutely neceſſary for the rider to diſcover and
" make himſelf acquainted with. A bad rider always takes off at leaſt the delicacy of
" both, if not abſolutely deſtroys it. The horſe will inform his rider when he has got his

CHAPTER XIII.

Of the utility of the Pillars.

The pillars were brought into ufe by Monfieur de Plefvinel, who had the honour to put Louis the 13th on horfeback, he has left us a treatife on horfemanfhip, the plates of which are valued by the curious for the engravings and the drefs which the horfemen of that prince's court wore. The Duke of Newcaftle, does not like the pillars, he fays " The horfe is tormented beyond " meafure to make him raife his fore-parts, in hopes of putting him upon his " haunches, while he is only put upon his hocks, he bends the hock but he " does not put his haunches under him to preferve the equilibre, he balances " his fore-parts upon the cords."

What gave this illuftrious author fo much difguft to the pillars, was that in his time the mafters made ufe of this method to raife the fore-parts of the

" proper bearing in the mouth, by playing pleafantly and fteadily with his bitt and by the
" fpray about his chaps. A delicate and good hand will not only always preferve a light
" appui, or bearing in its fenfibility ; but alfo of a heavy one, whether naturally fo or
" acquired, make a light one. The lighter this appui can be made, the better ; provided
" that the rider's hand correfponds with it ; if it does not, the more the horfe is properly
" prepared, fo much the worfe. Inftances of this inconvenience of the beft of appuis,
" when the rider is not equally taught with the horfe, may be feen every day in fome
" gentlemen, who try to get their horfes *bitted* as they call it, without being fuitably pre-
" pared themfelves for riding them : the confequence of which is, that they ride in dan-
" ger of breaking their necks ; till at length, after much hauling about, and by the joint
" infenfibility and ignorance of themfelves and their grooms, the poor animals gradually
" become mere fenfelefs unfeeling pofts ; and thereby grow, what they call, *fenfed.* When
" the proper appui is found, and made of courfe as light as poffible, it muft not be kept
" duly fixed without any variation, but be played with ; otherwife one equally continued
" tenfion of reins would render both the rider's hand and the horfe's mouth very dull.
" The flighteft and frequent giving and taking is therefore neceffary to keep both perfect.
" Whatever pace or degree of quicknefs you work in (be it ever fo faft, or ever fo flow),
" it muft be cadenced ; time is as neceffary for a horfeman as for a mufician.
" This leffon of the head and of the tail to the wall, muft be taught every foldier : fcarce
" any manœuvre can be well performed without it. In clofing and opening of files, it is
" almoft every moment wanted."

Earl of Pembroke.

horfe at once, before he had been taught to piaffe, by which the horfe certainly was put upon the hocks, and rather taught to rear and make points than to raife his fore-parts gracefully, but if in the beginning all idea of making a horfe raife his fore-parts is laid afide, and the pillars be ufed to make him perform the motions of the trot or walk upon one fpot, without advancing, backing, or traverfing, which is the action of the piaffe, it will be feen, that this cadence, which is eafier to be learned in the pillars than at liberty, puts the horfe into a fine pofture, gives him a noble elevated gait, and makes the motion of his fhoulders free and bold, and the fprings of his haunches elaftic and regular, qualities requifite in a parade horfe. Much art, patience, and perfeverance is required to train a horfe to this air, which the pillars ufed with fkill, will perform in a fhort time; but it is not furprifing that they fhould caufe many diforders when they are ufed for a purpofe different from that of attaining the piaffe.

A fkilful mafter has faid with great reafon, that the pillars give a horfe fpirit, becaufe the fear of punifhment roufes the fluggifh, and keeps them in lively action ; but the pillars have alfo the advantage of foothing thofe that are fiery and paffionate, becaufe the action of the piaffe which is cadenced, raifed, and fucceffive, obliges them to attend to what they are about. For this reafon I confider the pillars as the means not only to difcover the powers, the vigour, the lightnefs, and the difpofition of a horfe, but alfo to give thefe two laft qualities to horfes which have them not.

The firft thing to be attended to in the beginning is to make the cords equal and fhort, when the horfe is put between the pillars, in fuch a manner that he may have his fhoulders in the line of the pillars, and that only his head and breaft may pafs beyond them ; by this method it will not be in his power to pafs his croup under the cords, which fometimes happens. The mafter muft then go with one or two chambrieres behind the croup, and ftand at fuch a diftance as to be out of the reach of a kick, he muft

D d

then make the horfe move from fide to fide, by ftriking the ground, and fometimes his buttocks gently, with the whip. This method of making the horfe range from fide to fide, teaches him to pafs his legs, puts him in order, and makes him afraid of punifhment. When he is obedient to this aid, he muft be driven forwards; and when he preffes into the cords, ftop, and carefs him, to fhew him that this is the thing that was wanted. This is all that muft be required from him until he is confirmed in obedience to the chambriere, and will either range from fide to fide, or go forward into the cords, at the teacher's pleafure.

Some horfes of a temper naturally obftinate and paffionate, rather than range from fide to fide, or go forward into the cords, employ every defence their malice can fuggeft, do not piaffe but ftamp; others make ftops, and leaps, in the cords, repeated kicks, hang back, and throw themfelves againft the pillars. The greater part of thefe diforders is occafioned by the impatience of the teacher who punifhes the horfe when he does not deferve it, rather than by the natural temper of the animal. It is eafy to apply a remedy by being contented with making him range from fide to fide and go forwards for the chambriere; which, as has been before faid, is the only obedience that ought to be demanded from the horfe when he is firft put into the pillars. Another object of attention is, to make thofe horfes which are ftiff in the croup, and which cannot play their haunches, kick in the pillars; this action loofens the hocks, throws out the haunches, gives play to the croup, and puts all the fprings of that part in motion. But horfemen do not agree in this opinion, the greater part fay a horfe ought not to be taught to kick; experience however fhews that horfes never made to kick have their haunches ftiff, and drag them when they work, befides it is very eafy to break them of this fault, which affuredly would be one if they were accuftomed to kick from vice. As foon as it is found that the haunches are fufficiently unftiffened, the horfe muft be prevented from kicking, by being chaftifed with the fwitch upon the neck if he kicks when not required to do it. When the horfe leaves off traverfing, and will go forwards into the cords, he muft be encouraged with the voice and whip, to get from him fome paces of the trot in one place, ftraight and in the middle of the cords, which is called the piaffe, and immediately after he muft be coaxed and taken from the pillars to encourage him. If he continues for fome days to obey this leffon, lengthen the cords fo that the middle of his body may be in the line of the pillars; that he may have room to prefs forward more into the cords, and to raife his legs with more grace and eafe. Though he fhould continue to perform well, yet the exer-cife fhould not be made long until he is accuftomed to obey without paffion, and then it may be continued as long as his difpofition, ftrength, and breath will allow, and this without the help of the whip, but only from the teacher ftanding behind the croup animating with the voice.

To accuftom him to piaffe without the aid of the whip or voice, he muft be allowed to move of himfelf, whilft the teacher ftands behind him without making any motion or calling with the tongue, until he has entire-ly left off; then give him a fmart ftroke with the chambriere upon the croup. This correction will put his whole frame in motion, and keep him in fuch awe, that after he has been fome time accuftomed to the leffon, it may be prolonged as much as is thought neceffary, by ftanding behind him, without giving any aid, during all which time he will continue to piaffe.

When he is to ftop, he is to be apprifed of it by the voice, and accuftom-ed to the found *wo bob*, after which the perfon who is working him muft go from behind the croup, carefs him and fend him away.

This leffon muft not be practifed until the horfe begins to know what is required from him, and neither traverfes nor refifts.

When the horse is confirmed in the air of the piaffe between the pillars, then and not before, he is to be raised from the ground in pesades and curvets, by touching him gently before with the switch, and animating him behind with the whip. The curvet is not only a beautiful air of itself, but it makes the horse raise his fore-parts, gives the shoulders a more suspended action in the piaffe, and prevents stamping, a disagreeable action in which he only beats the dust by his precipitation; in the action of the piaffe the motion of the shoulder ought to be free and high with the knee lifted up and bent, which gives the horse much grace. To prevent the horse from rising without a signal, which produces disorderly leaps without rule or obedience, every course must begin and end with the piaffe, that he may rise only when it is required, and piaffe in the same manner. Thus working by rote will be prevented, which is a fault common in ill regulated schools.

As it is dangerous to mount a horse in the pillars, before he is accustomed to them, a rider must not be put upon him, till he is dressed and formed to obedience according to the principles we have laid down. And when he is mounted in the pillars, the same practice that was followed before the rider was upon him, must be continued; that is to say, the rider must make him range from side to side, and help him with his legs to drive him forward into the cords, by degrees he will be accustomed to piaffe for the hand and heels, as he before did for the whip.

The amateurs of horsemanship in Spain have a partiality for the piaffe, and are much pleased with horses that take this air, which they call *piffadores*. Yet they give their horses an inconvenient disagreeable pace, because they do not supple the shoulders, nor make them acquainted with the aid of the heels, so that the horses only work the arms, have not a firm and light appui of

the mouth, are not balanced between the legs, and confequently are not in that true obedience which is the perfection of the piaffe.*

CHAPTER XIV.

Of the Paffage.

After having given a horfe the firft degrees of fupplenefs by means of the trot of one tread upon ftraight lines and circles, bent and taught him to pafs his legs in the circular pofture of fhoulder in, made him obedient to the heels by the croup to the wall, and put him together by the piaffe which combines fupplenefs and obedience, the two firft qualities that a horfe ought to acquire to be dreffed ; I fay, after all this it is time to think of polifhing,

---

* " Never finifh your work by reining back with horfes that have any difpofition
" towards retaining themfelves ; but always move them forwards, and a little upon the
" haunches alfo, after it, before you difmount, (unlefs they retain themfelves very much
" indeed, in which cafe nothing at all muft be demanded from the haunches). This leffon
" of reining back, and piaffing, is excellent to conclude with, and puts a horfe well and
" properly upon the haunches : It may be done, according as horfes are more or lefs
" fuppled, either going forwards, backing, or in the fame place : If it is done well advan-
" cing, or at moft on the fame fpot, it is full fufficient for a foldier's horfe : For to piaffe
" in backing, is rather too much to be expected in the hurry which cannot but attend fuch
" numbers, both of men and horfes as muft be taught together in regiments. This leffon
" muft never be attempted at all, till horfes are very well fuppled, and fomewhat accuf-
" tomed' to be put together ; otherwife it will have very bad confequences, and create
" reftivenefs. If they refufe to back, and ftand motionlefs, the rider's legs muft be ap-
" proached with the greateft gentlenefs to the horfe's fides ; at the fame time that the hand
" is acting on the reins to folicit the horfe's backing. This feldom fails of procuring the
" defired effect, by raifing one of the horfe's fore-legs, which being in the air, has no
" weight upon it, and is confequently very eafily brought backwards by a fmall degree of
" tenfion in the reins. When this leffon is well performed, it is very noble and ufeful,
" and has a pleafing air ; it is an excellent one to begin teaching fcholars with.
" The leffon is particularly ferviceable in the pillars, for placing fcholars well at firft.
" Very few regimental riding houfes have pillars, and it is fortunate they have not : for
" though, when properly made ufe of with fkill, they are one of the greateft and beft dif-
" coveries in horfemanfhip ; they muft be allowed to be very dangerous and pernicious,
" when they are not under the direction of a very knowing perfon."

Earl of Pembroke.

that is of regulating him and making him work true in the air to which his difpofition leads him.

The paffage is the firft pace which regards juftnefs. We have given a definition of it in the Chapter of artificial paces, and have faid that it is a trot or walk fhort in meafure and time, in which the horfe ought to elevate his legs in the air, one before and one behind, croffed and oppofite as in the trot, but much more fhortened, elevated, and deliberate than the ordinary trot. That he ought not to advance or put down his leg that is in the air, above twelve inches before the foot that is upon the ground, in each ftep he takes. This pace, which makes a horfe temperate, is very noble, and fhews an officer to great advantage at a review or on the parade. The action of the horfe in this walk is the fame as in the piaffe, fo that to form a juft idea of them, the piaffe is to be confidered as the paffage upon one fpot without advancing or backing, and the paffage as the piaffe in which the horfe advances about a foot at a time.

In the piaffe, the knee of the fore-leg that is in the air ought to be on a level with its own elbow. This leg ought to be fo much bent, that the toe of its foot be raifed as high as the knee of the leg that is upon the ground; but the hind leg that is in the air ought not to be raifed fo high, for if it were, the horfe would not be upon his haunches. Therefore, the toe of the hind foot that is in the air, muft not be higher than the middle of the fhank of the other leg.

In the paffage, as the motion is more progreffive than in the piaffe, the legs muft not be raifed fo high, it will be fufficient if the toe of the fore-foot in the air be as high as the middle of the fhank of the leg that is upon the ground, and the toe of the hind foot be juft above the fetlock of the other. Several things are to be attended to in the paffage, fuch as the pofture of the horfe and his pace, whether in one or two treads, the time, the meafure, and the aids to be given by the rider.

The moſt able maſters agree that one of the principal beauties of attitude is the well turned bend given the horſe as he works, but this is differently ſpoken of, ſome will have it, that the horſe ſhould be bent in a ſmall degree, which is only a half bend, in which he looks with one eye into the volt, others that he ought to be bent into a ſemi circle, ſo as almoſt to look with both eyes into it.

It muſt be confeſſed that both kinds give gracefulneſs to the horſe, but in my opinion the half bend does not conſtrain the horſe ſo much as a greater bend, and it raiſes the fore-parts higher: in the latter poſture, or whole bend, moſt horſes carry their noſes too low, and bend their necks. Thoſe who admit the half bend work their horſes ſtraight from the ſhoulders to the haunches, or only keep half the haunches in. Thoſe who prefer a greater bend, keep the haunches in as much as the head, ſo that the horſe forms a ſemi circle from head to tail: this is what they call having both ends in, and makes a horſe appear more upon his haunches, becauſe he is cloſer behind: both theſe poſtures may be admitted, provided they are differently applied according to the different ſtructure of horſes, few being well proportioned in every part, ſome are too ſhort, others too long in the back.

Thoſe that are well proportioned, that is neither too long nor too ſhort in the back, ought to be worked half haunch in: to do this, keep the outer haunch a little in, ſo that inſtead of the haunches being quite ſtraight upon the line of the ſhoulders, the outer foot behind will ſtand in the place of the inner foot, by which half the haunches will be in, and this is what is properly called half haunch in: this poſture is very graceful, and wonderfully convenient, for horſes that are well turned, and have naturally an eaſy carriage; horſes that have ſhort backs muſt be worked ſtraight from ſhoulder to haunch, with a half bend only, which will make them look with one eye into the volt; for if they were put into a more ſhortened poſture, by bending them more and keeping both haunches in, they would be too much conftrained, and would not have free motion of the fhoulders. Horfes of this form often retain their ftrength, and thofe muft be put to the high walk in a pace that is more extended, than thofe that go freely.

In the paffage with both ends in, the head is turned in very much, and the haunches as much bent in as the head, fo that the whole body of the horfe is formed into a femi circle. This attitude was invented to contract long backed horfes, and to make them appear upon their haunches, as they could not appear fo graceful, nor put themfelves fo much together if they worked entirely upon one tread. This pofture is only croup to the wall reverfed: inftead of making the horfe paffage croup to the wall, with his fhoulders towards the middle of the manege; in the attitude of both ends in, the fhoulders are to be put oppofite to the wall, and the croup in towards the center, fo that he almoft defcribes two treads. Having duly examined which of the three poftures above defcribed, fuits the temper and powers of the horfe; the cadence of his air is next to be regulated. By the cadence of the paffage is to be underftood the motion of a trot fhortened, raifed before, and continued in equal time without retaining or preffing forward. This air, which is difficult to teach a horfe, depends both on the aids of the rider and the fupplenefs and obedience of the horfe, for which reafon a horfe muft not be put to walk with ftudied nicety, until he has been fuppled through his whole frame, and regulated by the piaffe in the pillars. Though a horfe be far enough advanced to have his airs nicely and juftly demanded from him, the firft leffons muft not be laid afide, he cannot be too much confirmed in them; therefore every time a horfe is mounted, let him make three turns, and let one at leaft be fhoulder in, followed by croup to the wall; and fometimes, if occafion requires it, let him be put to the trot.

To drefs a horfe to this graceful action of the paffage, which is the effect of a fhoulder free, raifed, and advanced, his temper and his ftrength muft be attended to, for example, horfes that retain their ftrength retain of courfe the action of the fhoulder, thefe ought therefore to be lefs kept in fubjection, and when they do retain from malice or any other caufe, they fhould be brifkly driven forward with the two legs, and occafionally with the fpurs; for a time the ftrict rules of the juft-walk muft be difpenfed with, to reclaim them and keep them in due awe of the aids and corrections of the rider; on the contrary thofe that through timidity bear upon the hand, muft be more collected, more kept together, and more fupported by the hand than urged by the legs and houghs: with fuch precautions either defcription may be kept in the true air.

In the paffage, the change of hands muft be made on two treads, upon an oblique line, and one fhoulder muft go before the croup, fo that the outer leg before may be upon the line of the inner leg behind, and that he may be kept in exact equilibre between the two heels, he muft not be allowed to make one fingle ftep through the fear of the rider's outer leg, unlefs the inner leg permit him. The rider muft know thoroughly how to ufe both hand and leg.

In the walk on two treads, and in the paffage, the horfe ought to make as many motions with his hind legs as with his fore-legs. It often happens that a horfe ftops his hind legs in one place, whilft his fore-legs continue in motion for two or three fteps, and are not accompanied by the hind ones, this fault is called winding the fhoulders. It is a ftill greater fault to ftop the fore-legs and keep the hind legs in motion; which is called tailing or twifting. As the rider looks before him he fees the pofture of the head and neck, and the action of the fhoulders, and it is eafier for him to regulate the motions of thofe parts, than to keep the croup and hind legs exactly equal, but he muft acquire the knack of doing both, that he may be able to regulate thefe diforders in proper time, which depends on the dexterity of the hand and the nicenefs of the heel.

F f

It muſt be remembered, that the aid, to make a horſe paſs his outer ſhoulder and arm freely over the inner, in the paſſage, requires dexterity, to catch the time exactly. The ſkilful Mons. De la Broue ſays, the rider muſt be able to feel which foot is on the ground, and which is in the air, and muſt turn in the bridle-hand, at the inſtant the fore-foot of that ſide to which he is going, or to which he is turning, is about to be put down; that when he raiſes the other leg, he may be obliged to advance the outer ſhoulder and arm, and ſlip it over the inner one. Great facility of giving the aids is requiſite, to catch this time nicely, for if the hand be turned at the time the horſe has his inner foot very high, inſtead of widening the outer ſhoulder and leg, it will widen the inner one, and if it be turned when the inner foot is putting down, he has not time to paſs the outer leg and ſhoulder freely.

It is likewiſe proper to obſerve, before we cloſe this Chapter, that of the three poſtures we have mentioned, into which a horſe may be put in the walk, two cannot be uſed any where but in the narrow limits of the manege, and for the pleaſure of the career, theſe are the half haunch in, and the two ends in, but when a horſe is kept in a high and noble pace, either at the head of a troop, or at a review, at a feſtival, or on the parade, this ſchool exerciſe is not to be required from him; on theſe occaſions he is to be kept ſtraight from ſhoulder to haunch, with only a half bend to the ſide to which he is going, to make him appear graceful.

CHAPTER XV.

The changes of hands and the manner of doubling.

What is commonly called change of hands, is the line which a horſe deſcribes when he goes from the right to the left, or from left to the right, and as this leſſon is partly founded on doubling, we ſhall firſt explain what is meant by doubling.

The manege, or place of exercife, ought to be an oblong fquare, and dividing this into other fquares, forms what is called doubling large or doubling narrow.

This doubling, whether wide or narrow, as the rider pleafes, makes a horfe attentive to the aids, and ready to obey the hand and heel; but the difficult part is to turn the fhoulders at the end of the fide of the fquare, without difplacing the croup. When the horfe turns at the end of a fide of a fquare, he muft form a quarter of a circle with his fhoulders, but his haunches muft remain in the fame place; in this action the inner hind leg ought to remain in one place, and the other three, which are the outer hind leg and the two fore-legs, turn circularly round it, fo that it ferves as a pivot. When the fhoulders have reached the line of the haunches, the horfe is to go on ftraight between the heels to the other corner of the fquare, and the leffon muft be repeated at the end of every corner of the fquare, except thofe formed by the meeting of the two walls; in fuch a corner the haunches are to follow the fhoulders upon the fame line that they paffed over in the angle of the corner, and at the time that the fhoulders are turned upon the new line. From the fquares at the four corners, and the middle of the manege, are derived all the proportions obferved in a well regulated manege, thefe eftablifh the order that is to be the guide in the changes of hands, either wide or narrow, in volts, and in demivolts. The changes of hands are of four kinds, the change large, and the change narrow, the counter change, and the change reverfed.

The change large is the line which a horfe defcribes in going from one wall to another, either in one tread or in two treads. The ground plan will give an idea of the proportion to be obferved in changing large. In two treads it is to be obferved, that in the paffage when the change of hands is made, the head and fhoulders muft go firft as in croup to the wall, with this difference, that the horfe muft advance a little every ftep he takes, which gives great liberty to the outer shoulder, and keeps the horse in strict obedience to the hand and heels.

The change narrow commences at the end of the first line of the narrow double, and ends at the wall in a line parallel to the line of the change large, as the plan shews; some horsemen very improperly confound the change narrow with the demivolt.

At the end of a change, whether large or narrow, the shoulders and haunches must arrive together, which is called closing the change; that is the four legs of the horse must be all upon the line of the wall, before he goes off to the other hand. In the plan the change to the right only is laid down, because it is easy to conceive the figure of the same lines for the left. The counter change consists of two lines, the first is the beginning of a change large, and as soon as the horse has reached the middle of the place, instead of going on to the same hand, he must walk forward a step or two, and as soon as his head is placed for the other hand, he is to be carried back in an oblique line to the wall he quitted, and then continue to go to the same hand as he was going before the change. The change reversed begins like the counter change, but in the middle of the second oblique line, instead of going to the wall, the shoulder is to be reversed, to go to the other hand, see the ground plan in which the reversing of the shoulder is laid down; so that when he returns from the wall from which he set out to the right, he is found to be to the left.

All these changes, counter changes, and reversed changes, are made to prevent horses from working by rote, which is the fault of those that work more from memory than from the hand and heel.

CHAPTER XVI.

Of the Gallop.

As we have already, in the Chapter of natural paces, given a definition of the different motions of a horfe, in the gallop, either to the right or left, and fhewn when he is falfe and difunited; it remains only that we now fpeak of the proportions of the gallop, and of the manner of feeling it, with rules to gallop a horfe well.

Three confiderable advantages may be derived from the gallop, firft to make a mouth that is fenfible, fecondly to augment the wind, and thirdly to diminifh the vigour of a horfe that is ftrong in the reins.

All horfemen agree that the gallop gives the appui, and makes the mouth; becaufe, in the action of the horfe in the gallop, he raifes his two fhoulders and arms into the air, and as he puts down his two fore-legs together, he is naturally led to take appui upon the bitt, and the rider has time to make him feel, at this inftant, the effect of the bridle.

The gallop augments his wind, becaufe, as the horfe is obliged to extend all parts of his body, the better to diftribute his ftrength, the mufcles of the breaft dilate, and the lungs draw in a greater quantity of air, which produces free refpiration.

The gallop takes off the fuperfluous vigour of fuch horfes as make ufe of their powers to form difunited leaps and jerks, which incommode and diforder the rider; becaufe, in the motion of the gallop, the fore-legs are at a diftance from the hind legs, and the back, being the higheft part of the body, is under the neceffity of finking, which of courfe muft diminifh the force of this part; this is to be underftood of the extended gallop, which is proper for all kinds of horfes; the united gallop would give them time to continue the diforder.

G g

It is a rule, admitted by all able masters, not to put a horse to the gallop, till he has been made supple by the trot, to such a degree, that he offers to gallop, of his own accord, without being heavy, or pressing upon the hand; and therefore we must wait till he is supple in his whole frame, till he has been bent by the shoulder in, till he is obedient to the heels in the croup to the wall, and made light by the piaffe in the pillars. As soon as he is arrived at this degree of obedience, whenever he is put to the gallop, he will perform it with pleasure; he must be galloped in the attitude of shoulder in, not only to make him more free and more obedient, but to break him of the habit (which is common to most horses) of galloping with the inner leg behind, wide, and out of the line of the inner leg before; this defect is the more considerable, as it is inconvenient to the rider, and makes him uneasy, which may easily be perceived in the greater part of those who gallop (for example) with the right leg fore most, which is the manner of galloping horses in the chase and upon the road. It may be observed that almost all of them hold the left shoulder back, and are inclined to the left; the reason is natural, because when the horse gallops with his right leg behind open, and at a distance from the left, the hip bone in this situation necessarily throws the rider out, and places him awry, and therefore the horse must be galloped shoulder in, to teach him to bring his inner hind leg near the outer, and lower his haunches; when he has been suppled to this posture, it becomes easy for him afterwards to gallop with his haunches even, and upon the line of the shoulders, so that the hind legs may drive forward the fore-parts, which is the true and fine gallop. Many riders do not endeavour to feel the gallop, though it is very essential, and for this reason it appears necessary to describe the way how this may be learned in a short time. I learned it from an old rider, who had great reputation in the chase. Take a horse that has been used to the road, and walks with a long extended pace, let the rider give his mind to feel the position of the fore-legs; to feel the position it is necessary, in the beginning, to look at the motion of the fhoulders, to fee which foot the horfe is putting down, and which he is raifing; to count in his mind one, two; for example, when the horfe puts down his left leg let the rider count one, when the right leg goes down let him count two, and fo on continually one, two. It is not difficult to count this motion when he looks at the fhoulders, the difficulty lies in the effential part which is to transfer a fenfation of it to his own thighs and legs, fo that by the means of the fenfation excited by the motion of the horfe's left leg, in his own left thigh, he may be enabled to count one, as he before did when he looked at the fhoulders; and in like manner two, when the right leg goes down; with very little attention, he will in a fhort time feel which leg is put down, and which is taken up. When he is quite certain about it in the walk, let him practice the fame thing in the trot, which being a quicker motion, and more raifed, is confequently more difficult to diftinguifh; therefore he muft begin in the trot, as he did in the walk, by looking at the fhoulders, and fo transfer the fenfation to his own thighs as before.

When he can diftinguifh the motion of the fore-legs in the trot, without looking at the fhoulders, he will very foon do it in the gallop, becaufe the putting down of the two fore-legs is performed in two times, as it was in the trot: as foon as he is fure of the gallop, it will be very eafy for him to feel when his horfe is difunited, for a difunited horfe has fo in-commodious a pace that even if the rider fit but indifferently in his faddle, he muft be void of all fenfation not to feel the diforder which this irregular change of his feat occafions.

Although more attention than fkill is required to feel the gallop, it is neverthelefs abfolutely neceffary for a rider who works a horfe by the rules of art; and that rider who cannot feel the gallop of his horfe, will never pafs for a good horfeman. Mons. de la Broue fays, that in the true gallop the horfe ought to be collected, and have a quick motion in his haunches; this definition refpects the manege gallop, of which we are now fpeaking. The chafe, or road gallop, which we fhall fpeak of in the Chapter of hunters, ought to be extended. This quicknefs of motion in the hinder parts, which forms the true cadence of the gallop, is acquired by the defire to go on in the horfe, the half ftops and frequent defcents of the hand from the rider. The defire to go on puts a horfe into a cadence that is quicker than his ordinary one, the half ftop fupports the fore-parts of the horfe, after he has preffed on a few paces, and the defcent of the hand is the recompence that ought immediately to follow his obedience, which prevents him from falling into the bad habit of bearing upon the bitt. When the horfe goes freely, is obedient to the hand in the half ftop, and does not put his head out of place on the defcent of the hand, then he muft be regulated by the united gallop; in this gallop the hind parts drive forward, and keep time with the fore-parts in an equal cadence, without dragging the haunches, while the aids are as one may fay only known to the horfe.

To produce this cadence and united gallop in a young horfe, his natural temper muft firft be carefully examined, to know how to put him properly to fuch leffons as are fuited to him.

Horfes that hold back fhould be put out upon long ftraight lines before their gallop is regulated, thofe that have too much ardour, on the contrary, fhould be kept to a fhort, flow, collected gallop, which takes off their defire to hurry, and at the fame time augments their wind. Horfes that are ftrong in the riens muft not be always galloped on ftraight lines, but fometimes on circles, as they are more obliged to keep their force united when they turn, than they are when they go ftraight forward. This action diminifhes the force of the reins, calls forth their recollection, and takes off their defire to pull upon the hand.

Some horfes, though ftrong enough in the reins, have ailments in their hocks, fhoulders, or feet, natural or accidental; fuch horfes are diffident of their ftrength, and generally gallop with bad grace, their courfes muft therefore be fhort, that their courage, and the little vigour they have, may be preferved. Some horfes make the motion of fwimming in their gallop, thefe fpread their fore-legs afunder, and raife them too high; others again gallop too near the ground; to remedy the firft defect, the rider muft lower his hand, and ftretch down his heel, by preffing on the ftirrups at the time the horfe puts his fore feet to the ground.

To thofe that gallop too low, or bear upon the bitt, the rider muft yield his hand, when the fore parts are in the air, and aid with the calves of his legs, fupporting them with the hand drawn near his body when the fore feet are going down to the ground, ufing no preffure upon his ftirrups.

A horfe ought always to be galloped on one tread, till he gallops eafily to either hand, for if he were too foon preffed to go fideways, that is before he has acquired fupplenefs and freedom in his gallop, it would harden his mouth, put him on his fhoulders, and hurt his temper. It is eafy to know when he is ready to gallop in the attitude of haunch in; when he is firft put croup to the wall, if he finds he is fupple enough and able to obey, he will take to the gallop upon being flightly animated by the tongue, and quickened by the outer heel; at the end of a few paces ftop him, carefs him, and make him repeat his leffon from time to time, till he is able to complete a courfe in it; all thefe leffons well executed, adapted to the nature of the horfe, perfected by the fhoulder in and croup to the wall, followed by the ftraight line in the middle of the manege to unite and regulate the haunches, will in time make a horfe free, eafy, and obedient in his gallop, which pace well performed, gives as much delight to the fpectator, as it does eafe and pleafure to the rider.

H h

CHAPTER XVII.

*Of Volts, Demivolts, Paſſades, Pirouettes,
and Terre a Terre.*

SECTION I.

OF VOLTS.

The maſters of former times invented the volts to make horſes more expert in combats with the ſword or piſtol, which before duels were forbidden, were much in uſe. They employed their attention to make their horſes obedient and ſwift upon the circle, to render them active, and more ready to turn upon their croup briſkly, and ſeveral times ſucceſſively, that a combatant might gain the croup of his adverſary, or prevent his adverſary gaining his own croup, by always facing him; it afterwards became an exerciſe of the manege, in which the haunches were more cloſely confined, to ſhew the ſkill of the rider, and the addreſs of the horſe; therefore it may be admitted, that there are two kinds of volts, thoſe in uſe in the exerciſe of war, and thoſe practiſed for pleaſure in ſchools.

In the volts which repreſent a combat, the horſe muſt not be worked upon a ſquare, nor on two treads; becauſe, in this poſture, the combatant would not get at the croup of his adverſary: therefore it muſt be performed on one circular tread, only half haunch in, that the horſe may be the firmer behind. As the arms are held in the right hand, which is called the ſword hand, a war horſe muſt be very ſupple to the right; but the manege volts muſt be made upon two treads, upon a ſquare, which has its four corners rounded by the ſhoulders, called embracing the volts.

This exerciſe on two treads, is derived from that of croup to the wall, after which leſſon it is uſual to begin to put a horſe upon the reverſed volts, which serve as the principle for performing the ordinary volts; as soon as a horse is obedient to both hands in the croup to the wall, reverse his shoulders in every corner, and keep him in this posture, along each of the four walls, until he obeys freely to each hand; after this, reduce the oblong square formed by the wall of the manege, to a square (as in the plan) by keeping the head and the shoulders to the centre, and by reversing, or rather by stopping the shoulders at the end of each side of the square, or at each corner, that the haunches may get upon the new line.

Although the head and the shoulders of a horse are to the centre when he trots in the longe, and he is widened upon circles with his croup out, it must not be supposed that those are volts reversed, though some horsemen confound them; the difference is very great, for when a horse is worked with his head in, and his croup out, the inner legs are those that are widened, that is to say, those that pass over the outer legs, which lesson we laid down as preparatory to the shoulder in, but in volts reversed, the outer legs ought to pass and step over the inner, as in the croup to the wall, and this is much more difficult for the horse to perform, because he is more collected and upon his haunches in this last posture. And this is the reason, why this lesson is not demanded from him, before he is well acquainted with the hand and heel, and goes freely to one side.

All the difficulty of volts reversed, consists in bending the horse the to hand to which he goes, in making the shoulders go before the haunches, and in knowing how to stop the horse at each corner, to let his croup go round to the new line; all which the horse will easily perform, and in a little time, if he has been, before hand, made supple, and obedient in the lesson of the croup to the wall; to which he must return, if he resists in the narrow square, to which he must be restricted, to perform what is called the volt reversed.

As foon as the horfe obeys, and goes readily, on two treads, to both hands, in large and narrow fquares, in the leffon of volt reverfed, he may be put to the ordinary volt, by keeping him with his croup to the centre, and his head and fhoulders oppofite the wall, at about three feet diftance from it; fo that the fhoulder may defcribe the greater fquare, and the croup, which is towards the centre, the leffer one; each corner muft be rounded by the fhoulders, carrying and turning the hand quickly to the new line, keeping the haunches in a firm pofture, whilft the fhoulders turn, but the line defcribed by the haunches muft be a perfect fquare.   By carrying a horfe, in this manner, to one fide, from corner to corner, he is never thrown down in the volt, nor does he work awry; the laft defect is very great, inafmuch as it lames the haunches and ruins the fetlocks of the horfe; defects which fome horfemen fuppofe to arife from volts in general, but doubtlefs they mean only volts awry, and tail-foremoft; for I believe, no intelligent horfeman can fay it, of an open air, well performed, which fo beautifully difplays the obedience and gen-tlenefs of the horfe, embellifhes his action, and fhews the rider to fo much advantage.   The able De la Broue who firft found out the juftnefs and proportion of the true volts, lays down an excellent leffon to prepare a horfe for this air; it is, to walk in the fchool pace, ftraight, and on one tread, round the four lines of a fquare, with his head placed in, and at the end of every line, when the haunches have reached the corner, formed by the meeting of two fides, to turn the fhoulders, till they reach the line of the haunches; fee the ground plan.   This leffon is fo much the more beneficial, as it keeps the horfe between the legs, and gives him great fupplenefs in the fhoulders; the walk, being ftraight, takes away all chance of refiftance.   The rounding of the fhoulders at every corner, teaches the horfe to turn eafily, and the haunches being kept firm and pliant in this motion, are employed to fupport the action of the outer leg and fhoulder.   The practice of thefe rules, fuited to the temper, by keep-ing a horfe collected on the ftraight line, that is heavy, or that pulls upon the hand, by driving forward him that retains, and by opening the fhoulders of both at every corner, places the head, and regulates the neck, the fhoulders, and haunches of a horfe, almoft without his perceiving the fubjection in which he is held by this leffon. That the fhoulders may turn with more eafe, and the croup be kept in order at the end of each line of the fquare, a half ftop muft be made before the fore-parts are turned, and after the half ftop, the hand muft be given, that the free action of the fhoulders may not be interrupted; the horfe muft be bent to the fide to which he goes, that his head, his fight, and his action, may be all carried together upon the tread, and the rounding of every corner of the volt. When the horfe is become obedient to this leffon, in the fhort fchool pace, he muft be taught to perform it in a more animated and higher pace, to prepare him to practife it in the gallop, and always in the fame pofture, that is to fay, ftraight from fhoulder to haunch, with his head bent to the way he is going. Every courfe muft end in the middle of the volt, whether it be performed in the walk or the gallop, for which purpofe the horfe muft be turned in the middle of one of the fides of the fquare, carried forward to the centre, and ftopped ftraight between the legs, and the rider will difmount.

When the horfe can paffage freely round the four fides of the fquare upon one tread, has acquired facility in galloping, united with a proper bend in the fame attitude, then he muft be paffaged round upon two treads, taking care, as we have already faid more than once, though it cannot be too often repeated, to make the fhoulders go firft, that the fhoulder out of the volt may have facility in paffing the outer arm over the inner, which is the moft difficult part; for, by checking the free motion of the fhoulders, the horfe would be thrown awry in the volt: when horfes are heavy in hand, or pull hard, their haunches muft be kept a little more in fubjection, to lighten the fore-parts, but ftill the croup muft not go before the fhoulders. On the contrary, thofe that have more lightnefs than ftrength ought not to have their haunches fo much confined, that they may be enabled to move more freely; let fuch therefore always be kept in a free and advanced motion. When a horſe is firſt put upon the volts, too much nicety muſt not be obſerved, for it may happen, that a horſe, which is naturally impatient, will throw himſelf into a ſtate of inquietude, that will cauſe many diſorders; and one that is ſluggiſh and dull, will ſuppreſs his vigour and courage; neither is it proper to put a horſe at once upon the volts, after he has been out of practice for ſome days, for as he will be very briſk, he may make uſe of his defences; ſuch horſes muſt firſt be put into the gallop upon one tread, until their livelineſs is abated, and their reins are lowered: it is therefore prudent, for a ſkilful rider, to give up ſome points of nicety, and to recur to the firſt rules, when any diſorder ariſes.

A horſe muſt be paſſaged on the volts of two treads, for ſome time before he is put to the gallop in them in that poſture; but when he is ſupple and eaſy in this attitude, he will take the ſhort gallop with a ſwift gliding motion of the haunches, upon being very ſlightly animated, which is the true gallop of the volts.

Redoubled volts, are volts repeated ſeveral times ſucceſſively to the ſame hand, but a horſe muſt have acquired a great deal of ſuppleneſs, muſt be well in wind, and thoroughly underſtand the nice proportion of the exerciſe, before he is able to redouble on the volts. A leſſon that is ſo violent might damp his ſpirits, and deſtroy his vigour; for which reaſon, in the beginning, the horſe muſt be ſtopped and careſſed at the end of every volt, to give him time to recollect, and to recover his ſtrength and breath, the hand and the place alſo ſhould be changed, to calm thoſe apprehenſions which the ſubjection he is under in the volts muſt create.

The change of hands, in the volts, is performed two ways, either without or within.

To change hands without the volt, ſimply place his head, and bend his body to the other hand, aiding him with the inner leg, which now becomes the outer one, and the change is made.

The change of bands within the volt, is performed, by turning the horfe upon the middle of one of the lines of the fquare, then carrying him, upon a ftraight line, to the middle of the volt, and from thence fideways to the other line, to place him for and to take the other hand; when this change is begun and ended with the haunches in, it is called a demivolt in the volt.

The fize of a volt muft be proportioned to the fize of the horfe, for a little horfe upon a large fquare, and a large horfe upon a little one, would be awkward; the mafters of the art have fettled the proportion very properly, in allowing two lengths of a horfe, for the diftance between the fides of the fquare to be defcribed by the hind legs, fo that the total diameter of the volt is four lengths of the horfe.

————

SECTION II.

Of Demivolts.

The demivolt is a narrow change of hands, with the haunch in, performed, either in the volt, or at the end of a ftraight line : a demivolt ought to confift of three lines; in the firft, the horfe goes fideways, twice his length, without advancing or backing; then his fhoulders are to be turned to the fecond line, which is to be of the fame length ; and, after turning on the third line, the horfe is to go forward a little, and the demivolt is to be clofed, by making him arrive, with his four legs, upon the line of the wall, to go off to the other hand.

The reafon why the horfe muft end the demivolt by arriving with his four legs upon the line of the wall is, that otherwife the demivolt would be open, and as the hind parts would be wide, and at a diftance from the tread of the fore-feet, the horfe would go off with the inner, inftead of both his haunches, which would throw him upon his shoulders; therefore, at the end of every change of hands, or of every demivolt, the horse must arrive straight, that he may be able to use both haunches together, to drive forward his fore-parts, and to be light in hand.

Before a demivolt, a half stop must be made, the rider throwing the counterpoise of his body a little back, to put the horse upon his haunches; the parade must not be weak nor disunited, but as vigorous and smart as the nature of the horse will allow, that the demivolt may be performed with an air of justness and vigour.

A horse must not be put to demivolts, until he knows how to perform complete volts, because, in a narrow space of ground, he might close and back; which cannot happen, if he has been confirmed in the passage of one tread, round the four sides of the volt. If he resists, he must be driven forward; and if he bears upon the hand, he must be reined back.

When he obeys, in the passage, upon the demivolt, he must be animated at the end of the last line, to make him perform four or five times of the short, low, and quick gallop; after which he must be caressed, and when the horse shews he is well disposed to it, than let him begin and end the demivolt in the same gallop.

Both in volts and demivolts, the order of the lesson must be often varied, by change of time and place; for, if demivolts were always to be performed on the same spot, the horse might anticipate the aid, and perform them of his own accord.

If a horse refuses to follow the rules of the proportion, and niceties of the volts and demivolts, put him to the shoulder in, and the croup to the wall: this will dissipate his passion, and diminish his heat. However, these disorders never happen to any, except those men who do not follow nature, but will harass their horses, and dress them too fast; instead of which the horse should be brought on by eafe and fupplenefs, and not by violence; for in proportion as a horfe becomes fupple, and underftands the rider's will, he becomes inclined to obey, unlefs he be of a rebellious difpofition, in which cafe no regular exercife can be expected from him, the utmoft that is to be hoped for, is fuch a degree of fimple obedience, as will make him perform that kind of fervice for which he is defigned, or which fuits his difpofition.

SECTION III.

Of Paffades.

The paffade, as we have already faid, in the Chapter of artifitial paces, is a ftrait line, on which a horfe paffes and repaffes, from which it takes its name, and at the end of which a change of hands or demivolt is made. The length of the line, ought to be about five lengths of the horfe, and the demivolt fhould only be about one length wide, fo that they are only half as wide as common demivolts; for as this exercife was formed for combat, when a horfeman had ftruck his antagonift with his fword, the fooner he was able to turn his horfe afterwards, the fooner he would be in a condition to return upon him and give him another blow. Thefe demivolts for combat are to be performed in three times, and the laft ought to clofe the demivolt; the horfe muft be collected and upon his haunches when he turns, to keep his hind legs firm and free from flipping. The rider is alfo more at his eafe, and better in his feat.

There are two kinds of paffades, thofe which are performed in the fhort gallop, both in the line of the paffade and the demivolt, and thofe which are called furious, which are performed full fpeed from the middle of the line of the paffade to the place where the ftop is made to begin the demivolt. Thus, in the furious paffade, after the demivolt is ended, the fhort gallop is continued to the middle of the ftraight line, as well to get fettled in the faddle, as to examine the motions of the antagonift, againft whom the horfe is impelled at full fpeed, and then collected for the other hand.

When the horfe is obedient in paffades along the wall, and can change his foot eafily, and without being difunited at the end of every demivolt, then the paffades muft be performed in the middle of the manege. As this exercife is formed for combat, it muft be performed at liberty, that the combatant may go to meet his antagonift.

Paffades are alfo performed in the manege, in which the demivolts are as wide as the common ones, and then it no longer is an exercife for war, but for the fchool, performed for pleafure, and to fupple a horfe that requires it. The line of the paffade is made longer, or fhorter, according as the horfe pulls, or retains, that he may be kept obedient to the hand and heel of the rider.

Although this exercife is as beautiful as it is difficult to perform, we fhall not here enter into further detail, becaufe the fame rules are followed in this as in the volts. If the horfe refufes to obey, it muft be from ill temper, or want of fupplenefs, in this cafe recourfe muft be had to firft principles.

SECTION IV.

Of the Pirouette.

The pirouette is only a volt in the horfe's length, without change of place; the haunches remain on the centre and the fhoulders defcribe the circle. In this action, the inner leg behind is not raifed from the ground, but turns upon the fame fpot, and ferves as a pivot, round which the other three legs, and the whole body of the horfe, turn. The demi pirouette is a demivolt in one place, and in the length of the horfe, it is a kind of change of hands, performed by turning a horfe from head to tail, with the haunches remaining in the fame place: Paffades and pirouettes, as well as volts and demivolts, are the exercife of war, and ufed to turn quickly, for fear of fur-prife, to get the ftart of an antagonift, to avoid his attack, or to attack him with advantage. Few horfes are able to perform many pirouettes, fucceffive-ly, with the fame degree of fpirit, which is the beauty of this air, becaufe there are but few that have the requifite qualities.

The horfe ought to be fupple in his fhoulders, very firm and fure upon his haunches; horfes that have the cheft and fhoulders very thick, are not fit for this exercife.

Before a horfe is put to gallop in the pirouette, he ought to make demi-pirouettes to both hands in the walk, fometimes in one place, and fometimes in another. As foon as he becomes obedient, he is to be collected in the walk, and whole pirouettes are to be demanded, in fuch a manner, that without put-ting the haunches out of place, the head and the fhoulders, after a pirouette is clofed, may arrive at the place from whence they firft fet out; by thefe means he will very foon be able to perform them in the gallop.

If the horfe, after he has been made fufficiently fupple and obedient, refifts in this air, it is proof that his haunches are not ftrong enough to fupport the whole of his own fore-parts, and the weight of the rider upon his haunches; but if he has the requifite qualities, he will, in time, make as many pirouettes, as the rider fhall think it prudent to require.

To change hands in the pirouette, the head muft be quickly changed to the other hand, and the horfe fupported with the outer leg, to prevent the croup from quitting the centre; but the horfe muft not be fo much bent, in this air, as in the common volts ; becaufe, if the head were very much in, the croup would be thrown out of the centre of the pirouette: Pirouettes are to be varied according to the difpofition of the horfe; fometimes they are made in the middle of change of hands, without interrupting the order of the leffon, which goes on as ufual ; but what fhews the obedience, and the juftnefs of the horfe, to moft advantage, is, when working upon the volts, to decreafe more and more, till the horfe arrives at the centre of the volt, and there performs, fucceffively, as many pirouettes, as his ftrength and wind allow him.

SECTION V.

Of Terre a Terre.

According to the definition of the Duke of Newcaftle, which is very juft, the terre a terre is a gallop in two times, on two treads, much more fhortened, and colle&ted, than the ordinary gallop; the pofition of the feet is different, becaufe, in this air, the horfe raifes his two fore-feet together, and puts them to the ground in the fame manner, whilft the hind legs accompany them, with a motion altogether forming a gliding low cadence, in which the time is marked by a play of the haunches, which move, as it were, with a fpring. To form a more clear idea of it, this air muft be confidered as a fucceffion of very low leaps, whilft the horfe always works clofe to the ground, and goes obliquely; as the haunches, in this attitude, do not go fo far under the belly, as in the common gallop, the a&tion becomes more gliding, lower, and more marked. It is alfo to be obferved, that in the terre a terre, the horfe refts more upon the outer than upon the inner legs, which are a little more advanced, and clear the way, but not fo much as in the gallop, and as the croup is under more fubje&tion, in an air that is fo clofe, and in which the haunches glide fo much, the horfe is wider before than behind, which puts the outer shoulder a little more back, and gives liberty to the other. From the subjection in which the horse is held by this air, it cannot fail of being violent, and few horses are able to perform it with all the regularity and precision that are necessary; a horse must be very nervous and well suppled to perform it; those that have less strength and practice than lightness and courage, are afraid of such nice rules. Horsemen consider this air, which is now very rarely used, as a kind of touchstone, by which they prove the skill of the rider, and the address of the horse. We must avoid the error which some fall into, of confounding this air with the pace of those horses that work low, and trail an indifferent gallop near the ground, without any gliding motion, which closes and determines the haunches to form a united quick cadence. For want of knowing the proper definition of every air of the manege, a person is often unable to judge of the capacity of a horse, and consequently how to put him to that air which best suits his disposition. This error of confounding the airs, which forms the ornament of the manege, is the cause of attributing to certain riders, whose greatest merit consists in routine, a degree of knowledge, which consists only in their own ill-founded self sufficiency, and the blind admiration of those, who bespatter praise, without any knowledge of the art of riding. As the perfection of the terre a terre is to keep the outer haunch closed, the square of the volts, performed in this air, must be much more perfect than in those of the common gallop in two treads; but care must be taken at the corners, not to let the inner hind leg go before the shoulders, for then the haunches would be widened, the horse awry, and he might give a jerk, by forcing the rider's hand, to extricate himself from this false position; care must be taken not to hold the hand too high, because the horse could not go low and gliding, nor move equally fast.

The faults most commonly committed, by horses, in the terre a terre, are to back, to rise too high before, or to drag their haunches; when either of thofe faults is committed by a horfe, he muft be preffed forward with the fpur, to correct him, to teach him to be more collected, and to quicken his cadence. As, in this exercife, the parts of the body are fucceffively worked, care muft be taken, to feel in what degree he preferves his ftrength and fpirits, to finifh the leffon before fatigue gives him occafion to refift: The rules to drefs a horfe to the terre a terre, are derived from a knowledge of his natural temper, and the difpofition he fhews for the air, which may be eafily found out, after he has been well and regularly fuppled, if in trying to make him perform it, and putting him together, he acquires the ftroke of the haunches, which was before mentioned; though he may have a dif-pofition for it, his ftrength muft be œconomifed, particularly in the beginning, by not demanding from him above four demivolts, which he will eafily perform, if he is prepared by the principles which ought to lead him to his exercife. In proportion as his ftrength and breath make him more fupple, and more difpofed to it, oblige him to perform four demivolts, that is two to each hand, and after this, indulge him by a gentle, flow and marked gallop, which will prepare him for the complete fquare, in the mid-dle of the manege; let him form two or three volts in his air, and difmount.

CHAPTER XVIII.

Of the High Airs.

We have faid before, that all leaps which are higher from the ground than the terre a terre, and practifed in the fchools, are called high airs, and that they are feven in number, viz. the pefade, the mezair, the curvet, the croupade, the balotade, the capriole, and the ftep and leap.

Before we enter, in detail, upon the rules fuited to each of thefe airs, it feems to me proper, to examine, what kind of horfe muft be made choice of, for that purpofe; what qualities he ought to poffefs, to refift the violence of the leaps; and the kind of horfe, that has not the neceffary difpofition, and qualifications.

A horfe muft have a natural inclination for fome particular air, and of himfelf take to it, to form a good leaper; otherwife time will only be loft, and the horfe difpirited and ruined, inftead of becoming a leaper. It is a very common error to fuppofe that great ftrength is abfolutely neceffary for a leaper, that excefs of vigour fome horfes have, makes them ftiff and awkward, which caufes them to exhauft themfelves, by leaps and jerks, extremely inconvenient to the rider, becaufe they are difunited, and generally attended with violent efforts fuggefted by malice. Horfes of this kind ought to be confined in the pillars, when a continual routine of leaps fufficiently punifhes their ill temper.

A horfe that is endowed with a moderate degree of ftrength, with great courage and lightnefs, is incomparably better; what he does perform, he does with good temper, and he holds out longer in the exercife; whereas the ill-tempered horfe is worn out before he is dreffed, by the violence of the remedies applied to conquer his rebellious difpofition.

Some horfes that have weak haunches, neverthelefs form good leapers, becaufe they like better to rife from the ground, than to bend their haunches.

A horfe may be faid to have the proper powers, when he is nervous and light, naturally diftributes his ftrength equally and gracefully, has a light and fettled appui, and ftrong limbs, is free in his fhoulders, fupple in his fetlocks, has good feet, and a good temper; thofe horfes have not a difpofition for the high airs, that are very tender, impatient, and paffionate; that are eafily heated and difturbed; that clofe, ftamp, and refufe to rife. Some even fqueal from malice and cowardice; when called to action, make diforderly leaps, which difcover vice, and the defire they have to throw their rider. Others again, commit faults, from having tender and bad feet, the pain which they feel when they, come down, prevents their making a fresh leap, which makes them very disagreeable to ride; therefore when a horse has any of the above imperfections, he is unfit for a leaper. One thing more is to be examined, when a horse of proper strength is found, to judge what kind of leap is fittest for him, so as not to force him to an air which neither suits his natural temper nor disposition.

When the air is discovered (before he is put to it) he must be suppled, and made obedient to the lessons we have already explained. We shall now go on to the detail of each particular air.

SECTION I.

Of Pesades.

The pesade, as we have already defined it, is an air, in which the horse raises his fore-parts very high, and keeps his haunches firm upon the same spot, without advancing or backing. Properly speaking, the pesade is not one of the high airs, because the hind parts do not accompany the fore-parts, as they do in all other airs; but as this air is a lesson, used to teach a horse to raise his fore-parts lightly, to bend his arms gracefully, and to settle him upon his haunches, which prepares him to leap with more freedom, it is put at the head of the high airs, as the foundation and first rule. It is used, likewise, to correct the defects of those horses, which in the mezair and curvets, raise the dust, by working too near the ground; for the same purpose, it is usual, at the end of a line of curvets straight forward, to make the horse perform the last very high before, and upon one spot, which is merely a pesade made to give grace to the stop, but still more to preserve the lightness of the fore-parts. The pesade must not be confounded with those irregular motions that horses make when they rear, although those also raise the fore-parts very high and keep their hind feet faſt; the difference is very great, for in the action of the peſade the horſe ought to be in hand, and to bend his haunches and his hocks beneath his body, which prevents him from raiſing his fore-parts higher than they ought to be; but in the action which a horſe makes when he rears, he ſtiffens his hocks, is out of hand, and in danger of falling back. Before a horſe is put to peſades, he muſt be ſupple in the ſhoulders, obedient to the hand and heel, and confirmed in the piaffe; when he has obtained this degree of obedience, animate him with the chambriere in the pillars, and touch him lightly with the ſwitch upon the fore-legs, at the time he preſſes into the cords, and advances his haunches under his body; if he riſe ever ſo little, ſtop him and careſs him, as he grows obedient, touch him more forcibly, that he may riſe higher. In all the high airs, the horſe ought to bend his arms ſo much, that his feet may be turned up almoſt cloſe to his elbows (which gives much grace) and therefore, when a horſe is guilty of croſſing his feet, and ſtretching out his fore-legs, which is called playing upon the ſpinet, he muſt be corrected with the ſwitch or whip, applied ſmartly over the legs and fetlocks. Another fault is that of riſing without the aids, the puniſhment for which is to make the horſe kick; and thus one fault will be corrected by its oppoſite. To prevent him from continuing this diſorder, begin every courſe with the piaffe. This variation in the leſſon, will make the horſe attentive to follow the will of the rider. When he is readily obedient, in the pillars, to the air of peſades, walk him at liberty, and then demand two or three peſades, on one ſpot, without traverſing; after the laſt, walk him forward a few paces more; if, in coming down with his forefeet, he bears or pulls, rein him back, then raiſe him on the peſade, and careſs him if he obeys; on the contrary, if he retains or backs, inſtead of riſing before, drive him forward, and as ſoon as he obeys the legs properly, make a half ſtop, and immediately after a peſade: be content with a little at a time. Since the beſt horſes always ſhew ſome ſigns of paſſion when put to the high airs, they muſt not be required to perform as many times of the air in fucceffion as they are capable of, becaufe it might deftroy the appui, and render them inattentive to the aids, in turning eafily and readily; they might alfo ufe the air to defend themfelves, by rifing when they are not required; they ought therefore to be fpared very much, and great care fhould be taken, that they do not fall into any of thefe vices, which might make them reftive.

SECTION II.

Of the Mezair.

The mezair, as fome very properly define it, is merely a half curvet, in which the motion is lefs detached from the ground, lower and more advanced than the true curvet, but more raifed and marked than the terre a terre. It may be eafily difcovered, in the pillars, whether a horfe has a greater bias to the mezair, than any other leap. If he is naturally inclined to it, when he is tired, he will, of his own accord, fall into a cadence that is higher than the terre a terre, and more gliding than the curvet; and when, by repeated leffons, his difpofition is difcovered, he muft be confirmed in this air, by ufing the fame rules as in the pefade; that is, every courfe is to begin with the piaffe, which is to be followed by the mezair, and fo alternately, ufing the fwitch before, and the chambriere behind. When it is judged proper to practice this leffon at li-berty, walk him in one tread, then put him together to go in the air, either in the change of hands or in demivolts, but always on two treads, for it is not ufual to go in one tread in the mezair and terre a terre. The moft ufe-ful, and the moft graceful aids, that can be given, to make a horfe go in the mezair, are to touch him lightly and nicely upon the outer fhoulder with the fwitch; and to help him with the calves of the legs. When the croup does not accompany the fore-parts properly, the fwitch muft be turned back, under the arm, to touch him with it upon the croup, which will make him work his haunches more brifkly.

If a horfe commits any of the faults that are common to almoft all that are dreffed to the airs, which they perform off the ground, fuch as either to retain their ftrength, to throw themfelves upon the hand, or to work of their own accord, without waiting for the aids, the remedies before mentioned muft be applied, and employed with judgement, prudence, and patience, which are all three neceffary for a horfeman. The proportion of the ground, in this air, is to be the fame as in the terre a terre; that is, he muft be kept in the exact fpace of volts and demivolts; for as thefe two airs have great affinity, and form a clofe and gliding exercife, the pofture of the horfe ought to be the fame in both.

SECTION III.

Of the Curvet.

The curvet is a leap, higher before, more marked and more fupported than the mezair; the haunches ought to beat the time, and to accompany the fore-parts in an equal gliding low cadence, at the inftant that the forefeet touch the ground; therefore the difference between the mezair and curvet is this, in the former the horfe is lefs detached from the ground, advances and quickens his cadence more than in the curvet, in which he is more raifed, more balanced before, and beats his haunches more in fubjection, as they fupport the fore-parts longer in the air. It is to be obferved, that in the gallop, the terre a terre, and the pirouette, the horfe carries his legs, one advanced before the other, both before and behind; but in the mezair, curvets, and all the other high airs, they ought to be even, and not advanced one before the other; which would be a great defect, called dragging the haunches. Besides the natural difposition, which a horfe ought to have, for the exercife, to go well in curvets, great art is neceffary, to drefs and confirm him in this air, which, of all that are called high airs, is the moft fafhionable, and the moft in ufe ; for it is a pleafant leap in a manege. Without being rough, it proves the goodnefs of the haunches of a horfe, and fhews the rider in a fine attitude.

This air was formerly very much in ufe, amongft officers of cavalry, who piqued themfelves on having dreffed horfes. At the head of their troop, or on a day of parade, they were feen, from time to time, to make two or three curvets ; which ferved to animate the horfe, when he abated the no-blenefs of his pace, to keep him in obedience, and to give him afterwards a pace more raifed, warlike, and light.

A horfe muft not be put to curvets, before he is obedient in the terre a terre, and mezair ; for a good terre a terre, and a true mezair, are more than half the way that leads to curvets. Horfes unfit for curvets, are thofe which are fluggifh and heavy ; alfo thofe that are impatient, unquiet, full of fire and heat, becaufe all the high airs augment the natural fire of a horfe, and, by fo doing, deftroy his memory and obedience ; therefore a horfe de-ftined for curvets, muft be nervous, light, vigorous, docile, and obedient. When a horfe has all thefe qualities united, and it is perceived, in the pillars, that curvets are his favourite air, teach him to raife his fore-parts well in pefades, then animate the croup with the chambriere, to make him beat with his haunches, and lower the fore-parts, that he may learn the true ca-dence, and the true pofture of the air. When he is in fome degree regulated to curvets, and can make four or five, fucceffively, without diforder, accor-ding to rule, let him be put to make fome at liberty, in the middle of the manege, and not along the wall ; for thofe that are accuftomed to rife by the fide of the wall, only work by rote, and are difordered when the fame thing is required in another place. It is not proper to demand many at a time in the beginning; but, in making the horfe paffage, and piaffe, upon a ftraight line, when it is perceived that he is well together, and in a good appui, demand two or three curvets, well raifed and marked; then continue a few more paces of the paffage, and conclude with a few times of the piaffe; for if he ended with a curvet, he would learn to ufe the air to defend himfelf.

To give the aids well in curvets, the hand muft be ready and active to raife the fore-parts; the legs of the rider ought to follow the time of the curvets, without feeking it, for a horfe naturally choofes his time and proper cadence when he begins to be adjufted. Above all, the rider muft not ftiffen his houghs, becaufe if the horfe be preffed too brifkly, he will hurry too much; on the contrary, the legs from the knee to the ftirrup, ought to be loofe, with the toe down a little, to flacken the nerves. The motion of the horfe alone, when the rider preferves his equilibre in a ftraight and eafy pofture, will make the calves of the legs aid the horfe, without putting them to his fides; but if he retains, they muft be applied more ftrongly, and then relaxed again. Curvets muft be adapted to the nature of the horfe; he that has too much appui, ought to make them fhorter, and more balanced on the haunches; and the horfe that retains, ought to advance them more; otherwife the former will become heavy and force the hand, and the latter will grow reftive. To remedy thefe defects, let them be often put to the fhoulder in, this leffon will preferve that liberty, which they ought to have, to obey readily in this air.

When a horfe performs curvets freely, and without traverfing upon the ftraight line, walk him upon the fides of the fquare, as directed for the volts in the gallop; prepare him to go in volts in this air; and when it is perceived that he is ftraight in the walk, and balanced between the legs, on the four fides of the fquare, let him, from time to time, make curvets, but not at the corners of the fquare; there he muft not be raifed, but his fhoulders muft be turned freely upon the other line, without difordering the

N n

croup; for if he were to be raifed as he is turning, it would harafs him, and he would back. When he can perform this leffon well upon the four lines, and is far enough advanced, and fufficiently in wind, to complete the fquare in curvets, then he may begin to learn to make them with the haunches in; to this end, paffage him croup to the wall, and in this attitude get from him one or two curvets in two treads; they are not made by aiding him when he is in the air, but at the inftant he comes down with his fore-feet to the ground, aid him with the outer leg, to get from him one time of the paffage; and then aid him with the calves of the legs, and raife him with the hand for a curvet; and fo on, firft one ftep of the paffage, and then a curvet; when he can go well croup to the wall, put him upon the fquare in the middle of the place of exercife, keep him in two treads, and accuftom him to rife in this air in this pofture, but proportion the leffon to his obedience and difpofition. The haunches muft not be kept in fo much, in curvets upon the volts, as in the terre a terre, or mezair; for if the croup were kept too much in fubjection, the horfe could not work the haunches with fufficient liberty, and therefore he muft be kept but little more than half haunches in; nor muft the horfe be bent fo much in curvets upon the volts, as in the gallop, or the terre a terre; he muft only look with one eye into the volt; and when he makes them ftraight forward upon one tread, he muft not be bent at all, but be ftraight from head to fhoulder and haunch; befides curvets upon the volts, they are made in two other ways, the crofs, and the faraband.

To accuftom the horfe to make the crofs in curvets, paffage him upon a ftraight line of one tread, about four times his own length, and rein back to the middle of the fame line; from thence carry him to the right two lengths, then to the left two lengths beyond the middle of the line, and return to the right to the middle of the line; there ftop and carefs him. When he can walk upon thefe lines forward, backward, and fideways, to the right and left, without traverfing, let him make one curvet at the beginning, one at the middle, and one at the end of every line; and if, after several lessons, he does not resist, then he may be put to perform the whole cross. In curvets, when the rider raises the horse in going back, his body must not be thrown back, but it must be kept straight, or even a little forward, though not perceptibly, to give the croup more liberty.

The hand is to be drawn back, to make him rein back one step, when he comes down with his fore-feet to the ground, and not when he is in the air. Immediately after this, he should be raised in a curvet, and so on alternately.

In the saraband in curvets, make two curvets forward, two backward, two to the right, and two to the left; and so on successively, forward, sideways, and backwards; it signifies nothing what proportion of ground is taken in this air; the horse may make as many as his disposition and strength will permit him to perform; but the rider ought to be perfectly master of his aids, and the horse to be well adjusted, and very nervous, to perform the cross and saraband, in curvets, with that grace and freedom which is requisite; for which reason, this manege is seldom practised, in modern days.

SECTION IV.

Of Balotades and Croupades.

The balotade, and the croupade, are two airs, which differ from each other only in the situation of the hind legs.

In the croupade, when the horse is off the ground with all four legs, he draws up his hind legs under his belly, and does not shew his heels. In the balotade, when he is off the ground with his fore-parts raised high, he shews his heels, as if he would kick, without absolutely kicking out, as in the caprioles.

We have already said, that art is not sufficient, to give a horse, destined for these airs, the proper posture of the legs in leaps; nature joined to art, and a natural disposition for the air, must prescribe the rules which are to be followed, to adjust them, and to make them perform the several exercises with good grace.

It is in the pillars that the air is to be discovered, and those that think to dress a horse to the leaps at liberty, before he has been suppled by rule in the piaffe, and without having studied his air in the pillars, deceive themselves; for every leaping horse, besides a natural disposition to rise from the ground, ought to be well acquainted with the hand and heel, that he may be able to leap lightly and in hand, when the rider requires it, and not by whim and routine.

When a horse, readily, and without heat, makes a few croupades, or balotades, in the pillars, at the rider's pleasure, then these airs may be demanded at liberty; following the same order as in the foregoing airs, but particularly that of the curvets. It is only to be observed, that the higher the horse rises off the ground, the more force he employs to perform the air; and that the art lies in preserving his courage and lightness, by demanding only a few leaps, but especially in the beginning. As soon as he has given some few times of this air, caress and dismount.

When he finishes a whole line of croupades or balotades at liberty readily, prepare him to rise in this air upon the four lines of the volts, passaging him on them, and getting a time or two of the air from him at different intervals; if he is found disposed to obedience, take advantage of his readiness, and let him perform the air upon each of the four lines, but not at the corners; there he must not rise as he turns.

It is also to be observed in croupades, balotades, and caprioles, that the horse is never to go on two treads, but only half haunch in. As his croup would be held in too great subjection, it would not be able to accompany the action of his shoulders; care must also be taken that the croup do not escape, at the four corners, when the fore-parts turn upon the new line; it must be fixed and supported by the outer leg.

The aids for the high airs, are the switch before, to be used to touch the outer shoulder lightly, succeffively, and not violently with heavy blows, as some riders practise, who maul the shoulders. To aid gracefully, the arm must be bent, and the elbow raised to the height of the shoulder. The switch is also used under hand, croffed over the croup, to animate the haunches, as we have already deferibed. Pinching delicately with the spur, is also of great use in the high airs, when a horse does not rise high enough from the ground; because this aid, which cannot fail of effect, makes the horse rise more than advance.

Although the horse is not to go in two treads, when he rifes in the high airs, yet he must be kept in this posture when he paffages or gallops; because in this action his haunches are closer, lower, and more in subjection, which makes him lighter before, and prepares him to rise. The faults of those who seem to drefs their horses only to make great efforts, which waste their strength, is also to be avoided; this is not the object fought after in a well regulated school. On the contrary, he ought to be kept supple, obedient, and regular, according to the true principles of the art; otherwise the school will be in confusion, and the equality of the measure, which ought to be obferved in every high air, will be interrupted. And this is a degree of perfection which must not be neglected.

SECTION V:
Of Caprioles.

The capriole is, as we have before defined it, the highest and most perfect of all the leaps. When a horse is in the air, equally high before and behind,

O o

he ought to kick out briſkly; at the inſtant of doing it the hind legs are cloſe to each other, and he throws them out as far as he poſſibly can extend them.

In this action, the feet riſe to the height of the croup, and the hocks often crack, by the violent and ſudden extention of the limbs; the name capriole is Italian, which the Neapolitan maſters have given to this air, on account of the reſemblance it bears to the leap of the goat, which in Italian is called caprio.

A horſe deſigned for caprioles, ought to be nervous, light, and have a good appui, an excellent mouth, large legs, and hocks, perfectly good feet, fit to ſupport this air; for if nature does not make him light, and give him a diſpoſition for it, it is in vain to work, he will never make a good leaping horſe. To make a perfect capriole, the horſe ought to riſe before and behind equally; ſo that when he leaps, his croup and withers ought to be on a level; the head is to be ſtraight and fixed, the arms equally bent, and in each leap he ought not to advance above one foot. Some horſes, in their capriole, come down with their four feet on the ſame ſpot, riſe again in like manner, and continue ſo to do, as long as their ſtrength admits; but this is very rare, and does not hold long; ſuch are ſaid to leap *in one time*, or *de ferme a ferme*.

In dreſſing a horſe to caprioles, when he is found to poſſeſs the qualities and diſpoſition which we have explained, after he has been made ſupple by the ſhoulder in, and knows the hand and heel, in the paſſage and gallop, he muſt be taught to riſe in peſades in the pillars; theſe muſt be made ſlow in the beginning, and very high before, that he may have time to raiſe his fore-parts, and to riſe without heat. When he can riſe eaſily, and high before, and bend his arms, he muſt be taught to kick with the chambriere, and the time to apply it is, when the fore-parts are raiſed high, and about to come down, for if it were given at the time he is rifing, he would only make jerks, and ftiffen his hocks. When he knows how to kick out vigoroufly, whilft his fore-parts are in the air, which forms the capriole, the number of pefades muft be diminifhed, and that of caprioles encreafed; and as foon as he appears to grow tired, leave off; for when his fpirits are exhaufted, his ftrength will be difunited, and the leaps will only be jerks and defences. When he is obedient to this exercife in the pillars, paffage him at liberty, and get fome times of the air from him in a ftraight line, by aiding with the fwitch, upon the fhoulder, when the fore-parts are defcending, but not when they are rifing up; when the goad is ufed, the fame thing is to be obferved; that is, to apply it upon the middle of the croup, at the inftant the horfe is coming down. In regard to the rider's legs, they ought not to be ftretched ftiff, but eafy and near the horfe. When the horfe retains, the calves of the legs muft be ufed, and fometimes even pinching with the fpurs, when he retains very much; the former gives the croup great liberty at the higheft point of the leap.

The rider ought alfo to hold the horfe in hand, for an inftant, at the height of the leap, as if he were fufpended; and this is called fupporting.

Caprioles upon the volts, that is to fay, upon the fquare which we have propofed for the rule in the other airs, are the moft beautiful and difficult of all the airs, from the great addrefs required to obferve the proportion of the ground, and to keep the horfe in an equal cadence, fo that neither the fore gain upon the hind parts, nor, which is moft common, the hind upon the fore-parts. As the motion, in the capriole, is more extended, and more diftant, than in any other air, the fpace of ground muft be larger, to give more vigour and lightnefs to the leaps. The horfe muft be kept only half haunch in, which renders this exercife more exact and perfect, and the feat of the horfeman firmer, and more graceful. He muft not follow every motion with his body, but balance it, in fuch a manner, that he may feem to move rather to embellifh his feat, than to aid the horfe.

Of the Step and Leap, and the Gaillard Gallop.

When leaping horſes begin to wear out, they take, of themſelves (as it were for eaſe) an air called the ſtep and leap, which conſiſts of three times; the firſt is a time of the ſhortened gallop, the ſecond a curvet, and the third a capriole. Horſes that have more lightneſs than ſtrength, may be dreſſed to this air, to give them more time to collect their ſtrength, by preparing them-ſelves, with the two firſt motions, to riſe better in the capriole.

Some horſes interrupt their gallop, by making leaps from briſkneſs, either becauſe they are ſtrong in their loins, have been long in the ſtable, or becauſe their rider holds them in too much. This is called the gaillard gallop, but this exerciſe ought not to be reckoned an air, as it ariſes merely from a whim and caprice of the horſe, which ſhews his natural diſpoſition for leaping, when it proceeds from briſkneſs, and not from remaining too long in the ſtable.

THE WAR HORSE.

The arts of war and riding owe to each reciprocally many and great advantages. The firft inculcates the neceffity of commanding the powers of a horfe with certainty, and has given rife to eftablifhed principles for attaining that object: Academies have been eftablifhed, under the patronage of the moft illuftrious princes. Thefe principles, regularly practifed, have contributed greatly to the regularity of military move-ments; and it will appear, that every air of the manege is practifed in the evolutions of cavalry.

The paffage, for example, gives a noble animated air to a horfe, at the head of a fquadron.

In teaching a horfe to go to one fide, you prepare him to gain ground, to either hand, and incline as occafion may require.

By the means of volts you gain the croup of the enemy, and return inftantly upon him.

Pirouettes, and demi-pirouettes, give facility in turning quickly, in fingle combat. And if the high airs fhould not have an advantage of that nature, they give the horfe lightnefs and agility in leaping hedges and ditches, with eafe to himfelf and pleafure to the rider.

It is certain, that the fuccefs of almoft all military actions depends, upon the uniformity and regularity of the movements of the fquadron, which can only arife from good inftructions; on the contrary, that diforder and want of unity, fo often remarked in cavalry, arifes from ill dreffed and ill managed horfes.

This affinity, gave rife to a degree of emulation amongft the nobility, to acquire proficiency in the art of riding; that they might have the honour, and fatisfaction, of ferving their king and country, with more effect. From

P p

thefe glorious motives, the ancient equerries have been induced to publifh rules to drefs horfes properly for war; and, in following their footfteps, we fhall endeavour to elucidate the moft approved practice. There are two points, to be obferved, in a horfe deftined for war; his qualities, and the rules which fhould be followed in dreffing him.

A war horfe fhould be of middling ftature, from fourteen hands, to fourteen and a half, and this is the height required as ftandard, in all the corps of French cavalry. He muft have a good mouth, carry his head fteady, and be light in hand; thofe who require a full appui, deceive themfelves, for fatigue will make him heavy in hand. He fhould have a good temper, courage, bottom, and good action; pliant and fupple, be attentive to the flighteft aid of the fpurs, and well down upon his haunches, that he may go off at the inftant, and ftop firmly and eafily; he muft have no latent vice, for fome horfes will perform very well, when in conftant exercife, but after laying by, or being rode by a bad horfeman, they will become vicious: fuch horfes require much attention, and they are only fit for the riding houfe; as it would be too much, to have the horfe to cor- rect, and an enemy to combat, at the fame time.

Biting, and fighting with other horfes, are the moft dangerous faults a war horfe can have; for in a combat, when the horfe is animated, it is not eafy to controul him.

When all thefe qualities, we have defcribed, are found in a horfe, it will be an eafy matter for a horfeman to drefs him to the manege of war, by following the rules we have laid down, to produce fupplenefs and obedi- ence, that he may obey the hand and heel readily. This will be moft affuredly effected, if after fuppling the horfe well by the trot, he is con- firmed in the leffon of the fhoulder in, and the croup to the wall; if he is taught to turn quickly, and with facility, upon war volts; that is to fay, upon a circle half haunch in ; if he is ready at going off upon the ftraight line of paffades, light and eafy, in collecting himfelf, at both ends of the line, to form demivolts to either hand ; if he is ready and quick in executing pirouettes, and demi-pirouettes. Thefe are the effential requifites to render a war horfe fupple and obedient to the aids ; but another effential point muft not be omitted, which is to familiarife him to the noife of arms, the report and fmoke of gun-powder, the founds of drums, trumpets, and warlike inftruments ; the fight of flags, colours, and fuch objects as may be expected in the field of battle. There are many bold horfes that tremble at the firft fight of fuch objects ; and though they have good mouths, and poffefs fenfibility, they lofe all recollection of the intention of the aids, as well as chaftifements, and abandon themfelves to the ftrongeft caprices, to fly the object of their apprehenfion ; fuch horfes muft however be kept in conftant exercife, for reft would renew their alarms ; and this proves that the moft fubtle art cannot totally overcome natural defects.

Mons. de la Broue fays, that the fhorteft and moft fimple way to accuftom a horfe to fire arms, and other military noife, is to fire a piftol, or beat a drum, in the ftable, every night and morning, at the time of giving the horfe his oats ; and, in a little time, this will make him as fond of the noife, as he was before of the crib.

Some horfes are fo very much alarmed, that they will ftart, prick up their ears, roll and turn up the white of their eyes, tremble and fweat with fear, keep their hay clenched in their teeth, without moving their jaws, and laftly, throw themfelves upon the manger or over the bars ; yet by patience and good treatment they may be reformed.

Another mode I have often feen, and practifed, is to put the horfe into the pillars, where, in a fhort time, and without danger, he may be familiarifed to thofe founds and fights ; fhew him a piftol, and let him fmell to it, beat a drum, or found a trumpet, at a diftance, and approach by degrees ; when accuftomed to this, burn priming, with your back turned towards the horfe, then go up to him, and let him fmell it, to accuftom him to the fmell of powder; this done, carefs him, and give him fomething to eat, and a little water; repeat this, till he is ufed to the fmell and fmoke; then load the piftol with a fmall charge, fire it with your back towards him, let him fmell the piftol, and carefs him. As he comes forward, put in a greater charge, and fire nearer to him, and laftly fire it from his back. With the fame patience and perfeverance, accuftom him to drums, trumpets, colours, and the clatter and fight of arms.

Horfes that are weak are generally timid, and thofe whofe fight is not very good, are difficult to teach. Though, in the end, fuch horfes may be broke, I would not recommend the ufe of them for war.

It is not only in the narrow bounds of the manege that this is to be practifed: the horfes muft alfo be frequently exercifed, in the fame way, abroad, and on the road, where they meet various objects, fuch as wind and water-mills, wooden bridges, and bridges made of boats. If the horfe be obedient to the hand and heel, and the rider know how to give his aids properly, patience will overcome thefe difficulties; above all, on thefe occafions, care muft be taken, not to beat a young horfe, becaufe the fear of blows, mixed with the alarm arifing from the object difliked, would totally deftroy his courage, and entirely break his fpirit. *

---

* " In order to make horfes ftand fire, the found of drums, and all forts of different " noifes, you muft ufe them to it by degrees in the ftable at feeding time; and inftead of " being frightened at it, they will foon come to like it as a fignal for eating.

" With regard to fuch horfes as are afraid of burning objects, begin by keeping them " ftill, at a certain diftance from fome lighted ftraw: carefs the horfe; and in proportion " as his fright diminifhes, approach gradually the burning ftraw very gently, and increafe " the fize of it. By this means, he will very quickly be brought to be fo familiar with it, " as to walk undaunted even through it.

" As to horfes that are apt to lie down in the water, if animating them, and attacking " them vigoroufly, fhould fail of the defired effect, then break a ftraw bottle full of water " upon their heads, let the water run into their ears, which is a thing they apprehend very " much.

THE HUNTER.

Although hunting is reckoned only an amufement, the exercife does not merit the lefs attention, fince it is preferred by kings and princes, to all others.

―――――――――――――――――――――――――――――――――――

" All troop horfes muft be taught to ftand quiet and ftill when they are fhot off from, " to ftop the moment you prefent, and not to move after firing till they are required to do " it; this leffon ought efpecially to be obferved in light troops: in fhort, the horfe muft be " taught to be fo cool and undifturbed, as to fuffer the rider to act upon him with the fame " freedom as if he was on foot. Patience, coolnefs, and temper, are the only means requifite " for accomplifhing this end. Begin by walking the horfe gently, then ftop and keep him " from ftirring for fome time, fo as to accuftom him by degrees not to have the leaft idea of " moving without orders: if he does, then back him; and when you ftop him, and he is " quite ftill, leave the reins quite loofe.

" To ufe a horfe to fire-arms, firft put a piftol or a carabine in the manger with his feed; " then ufe him to the found of the lock and the pan; after which, when you are upon him, " fhow the piece to him, prefenting it forwards, fome times on one fide, fome times on the " other: when he is thus far reconciled, proceed to flafh in the pan; after which, put a " fmall charge into the piece, and fo continue augmenting it by degrees to the quantity " which is commonly ufed: if he feems uneafy, walk him forward a few fteps flowly; and " then ftop, back, and carefs him. Horfes are often alfo difquieted and unfteady at the " clafh, and drawing, and returning of fwords; all which they muft be familiarized to by " little and little, by frequency and gentlenefs.

" It is very expedient for all cavalry in general, but particularly for light cavalry, " that their horfes fhould be very ready and expert in leaping over ditches, hedges, gates, " &c. The leaps, of whatever fort they are, which the horfes are brought to in the " beginning, ought to be very fmall ones; the riders muft keep their bodies back, raife " their hands a little in order to help the fore-parts of the horfe up, and be very attentive " to their equilibre. It is beft to begin at a low bar covered with furze, which pricking " the horfe's legs, if he does not raife himfelf fufficiently, prevents his contracting a flug- " gifh and dangerous habit of touching as he goes over, which any thing yielding and not " pricking would give him a cuftom of doing. Let the ditches you firft bring horfes to, " be narrow; and in this, as in every thing elfe, let the increafe be made by degrees. " Accuftom them to come up to every thing which they are to leap over, and to ftand " coolly at it for fome time; and then to raife themfelves gently up in order to form to " themfelves an idea of the diftance. When they leap well ftanding, then ufe them to " walk gently up to the leap, and to go over it without firft halting at it; and after that " practice is familiar to them, repeat the like in a gentle trot, and fo by degrees fafter " and fafter, till at length it is as familiar to them to leap flying on a full gallop as any " other way: all which is to be acquired with great facility by calm and foft means, with- " out any hurry.

" As horfes are naturally apt to be frightened at the fight and fmell of dead horfes, it " is advifable to habituate them to walk over and leap over carcafes of dead horfes: and " as they are particularly terrified at this fight, the greater gentlenefs ought confequently " to be ufed.

" Horfes fhould alfo be accuftomed to fwim, which often may be neceffary upon fervice; " and if the men and horfes both are not ufed to it, both may be frequently liable to

This preference is without doubt founded upon the affinity between the chace and war; in both there is an object to attain, fatigue to be endured, dangers to avoid, and ftratagems to practife; it is not then furprifing that an exercife which bears fuch a relation to the heroic fentiments infeparable from great princes, fhould fix the fafhion of their pleafures.

This is not the place to examine all the different modes of hunting; but the life of a beloved fovereign is fo precious to his fubjects, that it becomes our particular province to employ every means in its prefervation. We have already faid, that the chace has its dangers in common with war; but the great-eft part of thefe dangers arifes from ill chofen and ill dreffed horfes; for which reafon we have carefully endeavoured to find out the means of acquiring the knowledge of a good hunter, and the readieft and fureft mode of dreffing him to that exercife.

Many people think the method followed to drefs horfes in the fchool, is contrary to that which ought to be followed for hunters and troop horfes. This opinion, though badly founded, is the caufe of neglecting true principles; there is no guide left but the bad example of thofe who gave rife to this opinion, and perfevere in the practice.

The feat acquired is only a kind of fticking without grace, the execution is forced and without foundation.

How can any one, who poffeffes but a fmall degree of judgmen*, pre-

---

" perifh in the water. A very fmall portion of ftrength is fufficient to guide a horfe, any
" where indeed, but particularly in the water, where they muft be permitted to have their
" heads, and be no ways conftrained in any fhape.
    " The unreafonable rage in Britain of cutting off all extremities from horfes, is in all
" cafes a very pernicious cuftom. It is particularly fo in regard to a troop-horfe's tail.
" It is almoft incredible, how much they fuffer at the picket, for want of it: conftantly
" fretting, and fweating, kicking about and laming one another, tormented, and ftung off
" their meat, miferable, and helplefs; while other horfes, with their tails on, brufh off
" all flies, are cool and at their eafe, and mend daily; whilft the docked ones grow every
" hour more and more out of condition."

                                                        Earl of Pembroke.

tend to fay, that a rider, capable of putting in practice the principles of a good fchool, by which he is able to difcern the nature of his horfe and form his air, does not poffefs the art of fuppling a horfe defigned for war, and of making him obedient? or that he cannot extend a horfe defigned for the chace and give him wind? fince thefe are the firft principles of the art of riding.

It is very difficult to make choice of a good hunter, for befides the exterior qualities of other horfes, he ought to have good bottom, lightnefs, and to be fure footed. Thefe qualities ought to be natural, for art at the moft can only make them more perfect.

A hunter ought not to be thick fhouldered, nor very fhort in his body; becaufe fuch horfes are commonly fhort winded, and do not poffefs the fpeed requifite in a good hunter. He ought to be rather long in the body, to have his neck raifed, his fhoulders free and flat, his legs large and nervous, but not long jointed; he ought to be naturally fwift, fenfible to the fpur, and in a light appui.

Monfieur de la Broue fays, that horfes unfit for the chace, are thofe which natural timidity prevents from going faft for fear of running the hazards of the chace. Thofe which are diffident of their ftrength from fome natural or accidental defects, thofe which are by nature heavy and fluggifh, and thofe which are blemifhed, thofe which like better to make leaps than to diftribute their ftrength, and laftly thofe which retain their powers from malice and cowardice.

Though all thefe may be actually dreffed for the chace, yet they cannot acquire the qualities of good hunters, which are to gallop light, fure, and long. Thefe qualities are only to be found where there is a natural lightnefs, (which is perfected by the trot) free action of the fhoulders, and a light appui of the mouth, confirmed by the gallop, with fufficient wind and courage augmented by exercife. The trot, which is the firft rule to fupple all kinds of horfes, ought to be long and extended, rather than raifed; that the horfe may learn to throw out his arms and fhoulders; the bridon is excellent to give the horfe this firft fupplenefs; with this inftrument, which we have before defcribed, a horfe may be eafily bent, without being conftrained too much; he may be taught to turn readily and freely to both hands, without hurting his barrs or the place of the curb. He muft be trotted to both hands, without any regard to ground, but merely to vary the leffons; turn firft to one hand, and then to the other upon the circle, and fometimes ftraight forwards on a line of length proportioned to his inclination, either to retain or abandon himfelf.

He muft be kept to the trot till he obeys the flighteft motion of the hand and legs, and has learned to turn with eafe, readily, and freely, to either hand. When he is arrived at this point, let a bitt, fuited to his mouth, be given him; after which, let him be taught the leffon of the fhoulder in, not only to fupple his fides and to form his mouth, but to pufh forward his inward leg behind, under his belly. Which is a quality indifpenfably neceffary for a hunter, that he may gallop united and gracefully.

In putting him to the fhoulder in, he muft be kept collected, but not in a pofture fo fhortened as if he was dreffed for the manege; on the contrary, he muft be more extended, to give him eafe in throwing out his legs and fhoulders, but he muft not be laid out fo much as to acquire the fault of bearing upon the hand; for this, he muft be corrected by ftops, half ftops, and reining back. After the trot perfected by the fhoulder in, ftops, half-ftops, and reining back, he muft be galloped to augment the lightnefs of his fhoulders, to fettle and determine the appui of the mouth, and confirm him in the hunting gallop.

This freedom of the fhoulders, one of the moft effential properties of a hunter, is eafily acquired, if after he has been regulated by the trot, the rider knows how to extend his fhoulders and to make him throw out his arms, without the motion of the high fhort gallop, or that near the ground; by the firft error, he would be taught what is called fwimming in his gallop, and could not be laid out; by the fecond he would ftumble at every little eminence or ftone he fhould meet with, by moving too near the ground.

It muft be allowed, that nature feems to have formed fome horfes on purpofe, and has given them this free extended motion of the fhoulders, which conflitutes the true merit of a hunter. The Englifh horfes, above all horfes of Europe, have this quality, and confequently are feen to perform their courfe with incredible fwiftnefs. At their races held at Newmarket, the horfe that wins the prize muft run four englifh miles (about two fhort French leagues) in eight minutes, fometimes in lefs. Their hunters often run a whole day without being unbridled, and are always clofe to their hounds in their fox chace, and leap over all hedges and ditches, which are numerous in a country fo much cut and enclofed as England.

I am perfuaded, if fuch horfes as thofe were to be fuppled by the rules of art, they would gallop with more eafe to themfelves, and more agreeably to their rider; nor would they be worn out fo foon in the legs as they generally are; for in two or three years their legs tremble under them.

The reafon of this weaknefs, which does not appear to be natural, is doubtlefs becaufe the fnaffle is always ufed, whereas it fhould only be fo in the beginning to fupple them. As this inftrument is not formed to fupport the fore-parts, nor to give the horfe an appui, he is not helped in his gallop; and the weight of the rider, joined to that of his own fhoulders, neck and head, fatigues the tendons and ligaments of the legs, by which they are foon ruined, and the defect of ftumbling is produced. For this reafon, the ancient mafters invented the bitt, to fupport the action of the horfe in all his paces, but particularly in his gallop; in which, as he is more laid out, he is more liable to take falfe pofitions.

R r

When a horfe, intended for a hunter, is firſt galloped, he muſt not be galloped very much extended; becauſe, as he has not the habit of galloping light, he will bear upon the hand; neither muſt his gallop be ſhort; for that would prevent his throwing out his limbs as he ought to do; but he muſt be galloped united; without holding him in, or driving him forward too much; and juſt as if he galloped, of his own accord, without a rider. The gallop we ſpeak of is acquired by a light hand, accompanied by frequent deſcents of the hand. The deſcent of the hand, which is an exellent aid in every air, ſeems to have been invented on purpoſe for hunters, to teach them to gallop without a bridle, and without obliging the rider to ſupport them at all.

This leſſon of the gallop, muſt be performed on a large circle, firſt to one hand, then to the other; the courſe muſt not be long at firſt, for that would haraſs and fatigue the horſe, inſtead of ſtrengthening his wind and forming his gallop. The horſe muſt often be ſtopped from the gallop and walked, to give him time to take breath; and as ſoon as he has done ſo, put him to the gallop again. This method of changing alternately from the gallop to the walk, without ſtopping entirely, gives the horſe in time as much wind as his ſtrength and ſpirit admit of. The rider muſt be the judge of the length of the courſe of the gallop; when he perceives the horſe out of breath, he ought to put him to the walk; and he ought to ſhorten the duration of the walk, when he finds the horſe able to continue longer in the gallop. Another thing deſerving attention is, that at the end of every gallop, the horſe paſs at once to the walk, without making a ſingle ſtep in the trot, between the two paces; becauſe it is very troubleſome to the rider; and alſo, that he ſet off from the walk to the gallop in one time.

When the horſe begins to get wind, and can take long courſes in the gallop, without blowing or ſweating violently, then he muſt be put to the more extended gallop, which is called the hunting gallop.

In this, the posture of the head is not to be restricted to the observance of the rule of keeping the face perpendicular, from the fore-head to the nose, as in the manege; but the head is to be left a little more at liberty, that he may open his nostrils wider, to enable him to breathe more freely; but still, he must not be allowed to carry his nose in the wind; for he that gallops with his head high and misplaced, is more liable to fall, than the horse which looks at the ground on which he is about to put down his feet. There is a very excellent lesson that I have seen put in practice by able masters, to dress hunters; it is, to gallop in a large circle to the left, and to keep the horse bent to the right, united with the right foot; this method of turning to the left, though the horse gallops with the right foot, teaches him not to become disunited when it is necessary to reverse his shoulder, that is to turn short to the left, which would often happen if he were not formed to this motion, and occasion an irregularity, that would greatly incommode the rider, and disorder his seat. The old masters had a method which I greatly approve, that of galloping in a serpentine line; instead of a whole circle, they continually made sections of circles, turning the shoulders every moment without changing the feet, and so on. This makes a horse sure footed, and is easily practised where he has been properly prepared.

A hunter must not be confined to the bounds of the manege only, he must be exercised in the open country, that he may be accustomed to all kinds of objects, and all kinds of ground. He ought to be taught also to stand fire, and to leap over hedges and ditches; this is particularly necessary, that he may not be stopped by such obstacles.

Mons. de la Broue gives a lesson for this purpose, which I believe is both practicable and good; it is, to lay a hurdle three or four feet broad, and ten or twelve long, upon the ground, and make a horse jump over it in the walk, the trot, and the gallop, and to punish him with the switch upon the shoulder, if he put his feet upon it. After this, the hurdle is to be raifed about a foot from the ground, and as he learns to leap over it freely, it is to be raifed higher and higher, till it get to the proper height, and then it is to be ftuck full of branches of trees with their leaves on. This method, which he fays he has often practifed fafely, teaches a horfe to extend himfelf to leap over hedges and ditches ; but this leffon ought not to be taught, till he has learned to be obedient to both hands, to go off, and to ftop, and has had his head placed, and his mouth made.

OF CARRIAGE HORSES.

In former ages, magnificent equipages were only ufed for the celebration of triumphs, without attention to their commodioufnefs; but modern luxury, with incredible progrefs, has given rife to the conftruction of many and various defcriptions of carriages, and the moft common of thofe of the prefent day, infinitely furpafs thofe ancient cars.

The moft effential improvement, arifes from the carriages being fufpended upon the axis by delicate fprings, which render the motion almoft imperceptible ; and the lightnefs of the workmanfhip confiderably diminifhes the labour of the horfes.

When no improvement could be made in the conftruction of the carriage, more attention was paid to decoration, which has been fo fuccefsful that nothing is more capable of announcing rank and dignity than the magnificence of an equipage, if the horfes were better chofen and dreffed for harnefs. Negligence in this point, was pardonable in other times, becaufe the labour required to drag heavy ill fhaped machines neceffarily precluded graceful action. At prefent there is nothing to prevent our producing that elegant fuperb appearance feldom though fometimes feen.

Germany took the lead on the continent of Europe, and the example was followed by feveral French noblemen. It is however much to be defired that the cuſtom ſhould become general, not only for appearance, but to pre-vent thoſe accidents, which too often happen, in putting to a carriage, horſes that have neither been ſuppled, nor had their mouths made.

Enough is in general ſuppoſed to be done to prevent danger, by harneſſing new horſes, and putting them to the carriage, three or four times, before they are brought into uſe ; yet we have almoſt daily examples, to convince us, this precipitate mode is extremely inadequate to preclude danger, or prevent the horſes from trotting ungracefully, irregularly, upon their ſhoulders, with the head down, the croup high, or forcing the hand ; faults the more remarkable, in proportion to the magnificence of the carriages.

Let us now deſcribe the qualities neceſſary for carriage horſes, and the means of dreſſing them.

A coach horſe ought to have his head well placed, his neck raiſed, and to trot ſtraight and united in the traces ; he ſhould be from fifteen to ſixteen hands high, well turned, and high before, even though his back be rather low, which would be a defect in a ſaddle horſe ; he ſhould be full bodied, yet his ſhoulders ought not to be loaded, nor his breaſt too large, though theſe qualities would be proper in waggon horſes, becauſe they would pull better in the traces.

Coach horſes ſhould have flat ſupple ſhoulders, to be able to trot freely and gracefully ; they ſhould be neither long nor ſhort, but of a middling length ; for thoſe which are very ſhort, generally over-reach, and thoſe which are very long, preſs upon the bitt, for want of ſtrength, in the reins, to keep them up ; they ought to have clean well proportioned limbs, and a good deal of bone, but above all good feet. Great attention ſhould be paid to the hocks, becauſe coach horſes are more liable to have defects in them, than lighter horſes ; fetlocks that bend much, hinder coach horſes from reining back, and holding back as they go down hill.

S s

A well chofen coach horfe, poffeffing the qualities above mentioned, certainly deferves the pains neceffary to give him the firft principles of a dreffed horfe, fupplenefs and obedience: with thefe perfections, he will trot with more grace, and laft longer. Firft then trot him in the longe, afterwards mount him, and put him to fhoulder in; to bend him, give him a fine pofture, and form his mouth: he ought alfo to be taught to pafs his legs, by the croup to the wall, that he may make his turnings with more eafe; for every time a coach horfe turns, he defcribes on two treads, a circular line with his haunches and fhoulders, which is a kind of demivolt, and to perform this, he ought to know how to pafs his legs freely, both before and behind, otherwife he would ftrike them againft each other, ftrain his haunches, or turn awkwardly; he ought to be taught to piaffe perfectly well in the pillars, after he has been fuppled in the trot; for nothing gives a coach horfe a finer air, than the piaffe in the pillars. The pillars make him ftand in awe of the whip, and obedient to the flighteft motions of that aid.

Another thing, which is however feldom feen, is that a coach horfe ought to be bent to the hand to which he is to go, the off horfe to the right, and the near horfe to the left; this pofture makes him appear more graceful, enables him to fee his road, keeps his croup upon the line of the fhoulders, and makes him trot firm and united. Thofe which do not trot in this pofture, put their heads down towards the pole, which throws the croup out againft the traces, or elfe they ftretch out their nofes and pull upon the hand; which is the more dangerous, becaufe they have it in their power to force the coachman's hand, which is vulgarly called taking the bitt in their teeth, by which thofe in the carriage, and people on foot, are alike expofed to the danger of their lives. It is very common to fee one horfe in a coach lower his nofe, and the other raife it, which is both difagreeable and difcordant, and could not happen if they had been properly broke. If any one fhould be furprifed that I recommend the fame principles for coach horfes as for thofe of the manege,

I only-defire he will look at the equipage of thofe gentlemen who are attentive to their horfes, and he will inftantly perceive the difference between horfes that are dreffed, and thofe that are not. I do not fay that a coach horfe fhould be confirmed in obedience to the hand and heel, like a maneged horfe, but only that he be unftiffened, and have his mouth made, be taught to piaffe, fear the whip, and obey its flighteft motion; nor do I recommend thefe rules for all coach horfes, but only for fuch as from figure and price are worthy of this attention; clumfy, ill made horfes, may be left to the care of the coachman.

Pl. 1.

The WALK.

The TROT.

Pl. 1.

Pl. 4.

The AMBLE.

The AUBIN.

Pl.5.

The SCHOOL WALK.

The School, or Short, GALLOP.

Pl. 6.

The VOLTE *to the* Right.

The PIROUETTE *to the* Left.

The TERRE-A-TERRE.

The MEZAIR.

Pl.8.

The PESADE.

The CURVET.

Pl. 9.

The BALOT-ADE.

The CROUPADE.

Pl. 10.

The CABRIOLE.

The PIAFFRE in the Pillars.

Pl.11.

The SHOULDER-IN.

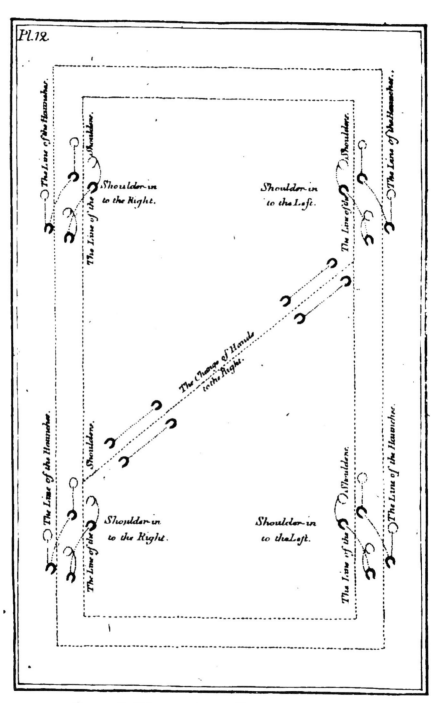

Ground Plan of the SHOULDER-IN.

Pl. 13.

The CROUP-TO-THE-WALL.

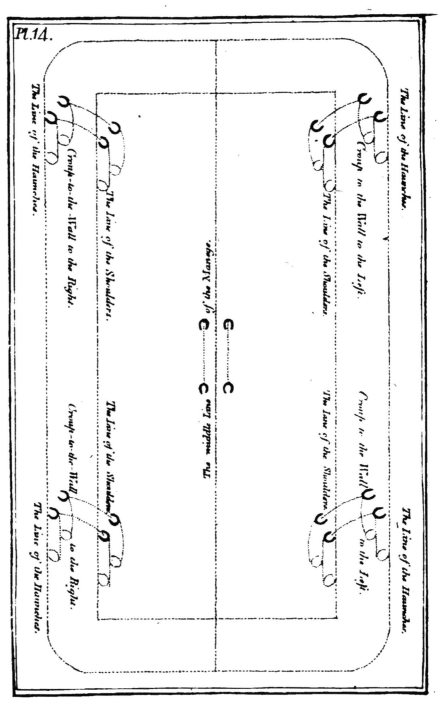

Pl.14.

The Line of the Haunches.

Croup in the Wall to the Left.

The Line of the Shoulders.

The Line of the Shoulders.

of the Mange.

The middle Line

Croup to the Wall to the Right.

The Line of the Shoulders.

Croup to the Wall to the Right.

The Line of the Haunches.

The Line of the Haunches.

Croup to the Wall to the Left.

The Line of the Shoulders.

The Line of the Haunches.

Plan of CROUP-TO-THE-WALL.

Pl. 15.

The PIAFFER.

Pl. 16.

The PASSAGE.

Pl. 17.

CHANGES OF HANDS.

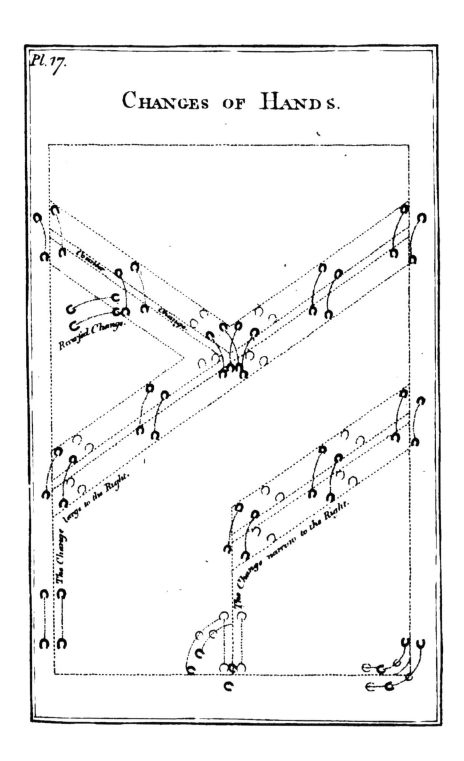

Pl.18.

The DOUBLING.

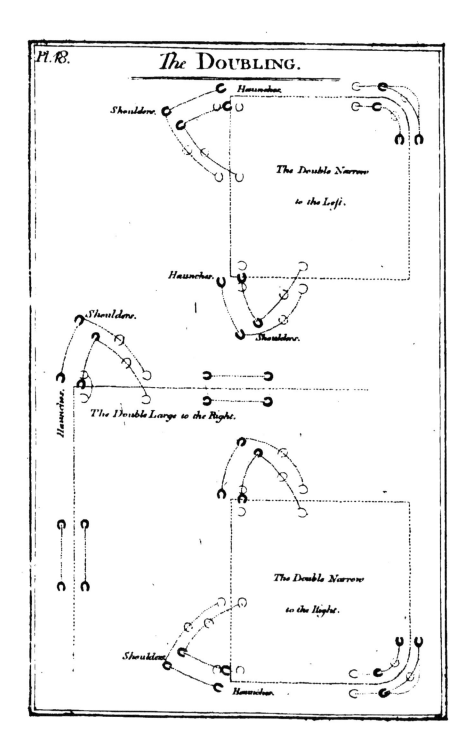

Haunches.

Shoulders.

The Double Narrow

to the Left.

Haunches.

Shoulders.

Shoulders.

Haunches.

The Double Large to the Right.

The Double Narrow

to the Right.

Shoulders.

Haunches.

Pl. 19.

The SCHOOL GALLOP.

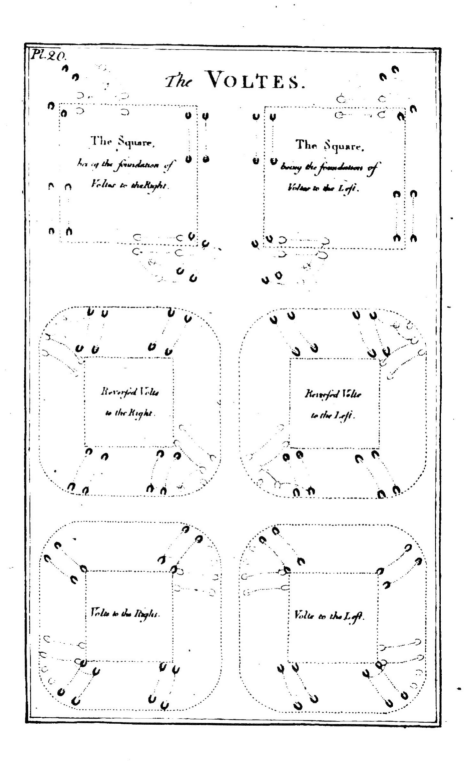

Pl. 20.

The VOLTES.

The Square,

being the foundation of

Voltes to the Right.

The Square,

being the foundation of

Voltes to the Left.

Reversed Volts

to the Right.

Reversed Volts

to the Left.

Volts to the Right.

Volts to the Left.

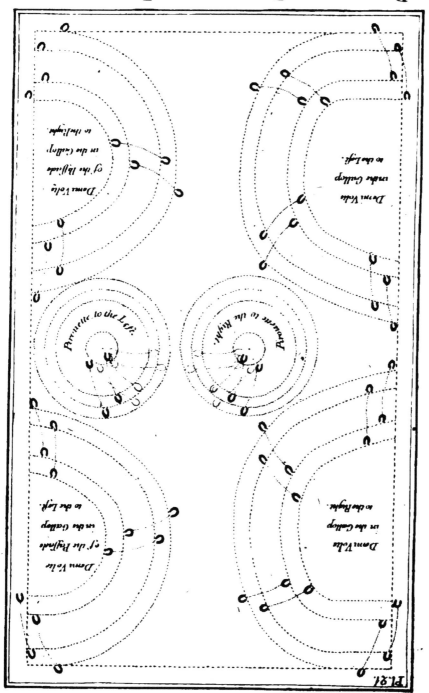

Pl. 21.

*Pl.*22.

The CURVET.